MAGIC CITY
Cravings

MAGIC CITY Cravings

The Most Requested Recipes from Birmingham Restaurants

Then & Now

Food Network Star Martie Duncan
with Chanda Temple
Foreword by Taylor Hicks

On the Cover:
Clockwise from top left: Bottega Bowl from Bottega Café (page 104), Steel City Pops (page 194), Chez Fonfon Coconut Cake (page 80), Jinsei Blackberry Mojito (page 56), Full Moon BBQ Half Moon Cookies (page 200), Momos from Bamboo on 2nd (page 78), Jim 'N Nick's Bar-B-Q Rub (page 164), and Shindig's Grass-Fed Beef Willis Burger (page 148)

Disclaimer:
Recipes are submitted by the restaurants and chefs indicated and may not be reproduced or reprinted without written permission. Images may not be used without written permission.

Published By:
Advanced Central Services Southeast

Copyright © 2017 Advanced Central Services Southeast. All rights reserved.

Reviewers and writers of magazine and newspaper articles may quote from this book, with attribution, as needed for their work. Otherwise, no part of this book may be reproduced in any form or by any means, electronic or mechanical, including photocopying, recording, or by any information storage and retrieval system, without written permission of the publisher and author.

Library of Congress Control Number: 2016947297

ISBN: 9781575714721

To order copies of this book, please contact:
Advanced Central Services Southeast
Carl Bates
1731 1st Avenue North
Birmingham, Alabama 35203
cbates@acsal.com
205-325-2237

Photo: Arden Photography

The world is discovering what those of us who call Birmingham home have always known: Our restaurant scene and the food found here are exceptional.

Birmingham is jam-packed with restaurants we love and food we crave. The Magic City has finally started to receive the national recognition it has long deserved as a top food destination. Readers at Zagat, the culinary travel guide voted Birmingham the No. 1 up-and-coming restaurant city in a 2016 poll, and the James Beard Foundation has honored Highlands Bar and Grill as one of the top restaurants in the country for the past 9 years in a row. (Quotes from the press about Birmingham food are found on page 4.) Birmingham also has a long and fascinating food history filled with dishes that became so legendary that they have a fan following decades after the restaurants serving them have closed.

I've had a long love affair with Birmingham food. My earliest food memories are of family outings to the Polar Bear Spinning Wheel in Wahouma, the Pioneer Cafeteria in Roebuck, and Andrew's BBQ in East Lake where I'd sit at the counter with an icy cold Coca-Cola and wait for my mom's order. Later, Cobb Lane was the only place my friends and I would go to celebrate a birthday or bridal shower, mainly for the She-Crab Soup, yeast rolls, and Chocolate Roulage. Sometime in the '80s, family gatherings moved to The Pita Stop, where the waiters know me and bring the Combination Platter with extra falafel to the table before I even ask. (Find the recipe for their Hummus on page 88.)

Later in life, I became obsessed with Highland's Stone Ground Baked Grits; it's still on the menu and still just as delicious as it was when I discovered it in the late '80s. In the '90s, many a date night started with a glass of wine and the Hot and Hot Tomato Salad, a dish so famous that Birmingham diners anxiously await the email announcing its arrival each spring. Today my cravings seem to center around sweets. If you follow my Instagram feed (@MartieDuncan), you'll see that I'm completely addicted to the coconut cake from Chez Fonfon, buttermilk popsicles from Steel City Pops, and just about anything Big Spoon Creamery stuffs between two cookies.

My first book, *Birmingham's Best Bites*, was written with Chanda Temple in 2014 as a love letter to my hometown. The "Days Gone By" section of the book was so popular that we decided to delve deeper into Birmingham's food roots this time. We turned to social media and posed the question: What are your favorite dishes from Birmingham restaurants—the ones you absolutely crave and miss most from area restaurants that have closed? Armed with a long list of requests, we set out to find as many of those recipes as possible.

Some of the recipes included in *Magic City Cravings* are simple and some are complex, but they all were requested from fans near and far who remember them fondly.

Magic City Cravings will raise funds for Children's of Alabama, and we owe a huge thank you to our sponsor Alagasco and to our contributors for making it possible. If the beautiful photographs within these pages do not inspire you to cook, I hope they will inspire you to make a reservation.

To the hard-working Birmingham restaurant families past and present—the front of the house, the back of the house, the farmers, the suppliers, and all who make dining in the Magic City so completely "craveable"—this book is dedicated to your hard work, creativity, tireless service, and commitment to your product. Thank you.

To those who collaborated with us to share your family's story and food history, thank you for helping us turn back the clock and relive the past through wonderful memories, family photographs, and treasured recipes. Your restaurants may be gone, but they will never be forgotten.

Martie

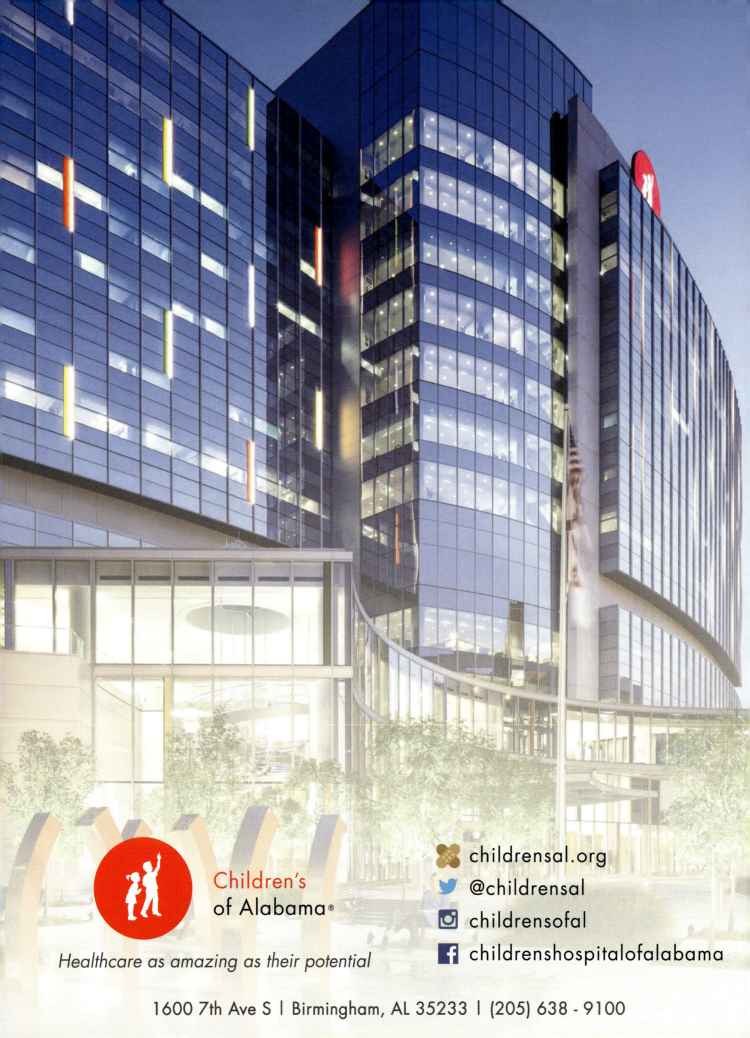

TABLE OF CONTENTS

5 Foreword

7 Birmingham's James Beard Winners & Nominees

8 Neighborhood Directory

10 Birmingham Then & Now

24 Gone But Not Forgotten Favorites

50 Cocktails

76 Appetizers & Breads

100 Salads & Sides

126 Soups & Sandwiches

152 Main Courses

192 Desserts

222 Restaurant Index

224 Recipe Index

226 Ingredient Index

232 Where to Eat What

234 Contributors

THE MAGIC CITY IN NATIONAL MEDIA

Birmingham? Yes, Birmingham. The breakout market from our survey ranked as the most-improved dining scene in the country over the past five years, hit high marks for a talented roster of chefs and is one that is expected to continue its stellar upward trajectory. It's safe to say that its dining and drinking culture has never been more exciting.
-**"America's Next Hot Food Cities,"** Zagat

Birmingham has long been an esteemed culinary destination with a deeply rooted farm-to-table ethos and multiple Beard award-winning chefs like Frank Stitt (Highlands Bar & Grill) and his former pupil Chris Hastings (Hot and Hot Fish Club). Many young cooks have spent time in their impressive kitchens, learning the ropes and as a result, the Southern city has become an incubator for burgeoning culinary talent.
-**"The 26 Hottest Food Cities of 2016,"** Zagat

Birmingham's culinary landscape reps the Deep South with the force of 1,000 crimson tides — and it's not all fried green tomatoes these days. Rising in tandem with its music and art cred, the Magic City's restaurant scene truly has something for everyone, whether it's white tablecloth award-winners like Hot and Hot Fish Club, Cafe Dupont, and Highlands Bar & Grill, date-worthy burger joints (Chez Fonfon will change your life, no joke), wood-fired pizza and craft beer at Post Office Pies and Slice, food trucks galore, or piles and piles of fall-off-the-bone barbecue (see: Miss Myra's, Jim 'N Nick's, Saw's). We hear the secret's still in the sauce, though.
-**"The Best Food City in Every State,"** Thrillist.com

Birmingham's nickname, "The Pittsburgh of the South," seems apt anew, thanks to the revitalization of the Avondale neighborhood, where artists, restaurateurs and young entrepreneurs are taking over brick warehouses and Queen Anne cottages. Since the neighborhood's eponymous brewery took up residence inside a 19th-century firehouse, hip hangouts like the wood-fired pizzeria Post Office Pies, the live music venue Saturn and the garage-turned-brunch hot spot Rowe's Service Station have followed suit, with mainstays like Saw's Soul Kitchen still dishing it out.
-**"52 Places To Go in 2017,"** *The New York Times*

"Downtown and its contiguous neighborhoods—Pepper Place, Avondale, Lakeview—are percolating with energy," (Hot and Hot Fish Club Chef Chris) Hastings says. "They're having a transformational moment." As you stroll through the concrete-clad grid, that energy is palpable, and the question locals most frequently ask is "Hey, have you tried that place yet?" As (St. Paul and the Broken Bones' Paul) Janeway sings, for Birmingham, it is indeed time.
-**"The Magic City's Next Act,"** *Garden & Gun*

foreword

While Birmingham is still home for me, I spend a lot of time traveling the country, and I've eaten a lot of great food. No matter where I go, I'm always happy to get back and hit some of my favorite spots around town.

The veggie plate at Niki's West always tastes like home to me. I've said many times that the Crab Cakes at Fox Valley or the Chicken Scaloppini at Bottega Café are Birmingham dishes I crave when I'm out on the road.

I'm always down for a slice and a cold one at Post Office Pies in Avondale; next door is Avondale Brewery, and Saturn is right across the street. Both are killer live music venues that you won't want to miss if you are in the neighborhood.

The drive out to The Bright Star in Bessemer always ends with a slice of mile-high chocolate pie—that's been my favorite since I was a kid.

Food traditions run deep in our city and folks will argue as passionately about where to find the best BBQ as they will about who's going to win this year's Iron Bowl.

The recipes found in *Magic City Cravings* will help bring Birmingham food to those with ties to the city who can't get back home as often as they'd like; folks can have Ted's Famous Greek Souvlakia or the Hot and Hot Tomato Salad no matter where they live. Like our city, these recipes are as varied as the neighborhoods and people found here. It tells the story of today's Birmingham where you'll find Greek, Italian, Indian, Lebanese, Mexican, Asian, and British cuisine alongside the traditional soul food, southern favorites, and barbecue.

The fact that this book raises funds for Children's of Alabama is reason enough to buy it. There is something for everyone within the pages. The neighborhood guides, insider tips, and Martie's menu suggestions make *Magic City Cravings* more than just a cookbook for a cause; it is a culinary tour of our home we can share with the world.

With love and soul
from my hometown,

Taylor Hicks is a soul singer from Birmingham who won the fifth season of American Idol. Since winning Idol, Taylor has produced several albums, appeared on Broadway, headlined a residency in Las Vegas, and appeared on television shows, including *Late Night with Jimmy Fallon*, *Law and Order SVU*, and *Hell's Kitchen*. In 2016, Taylor premiered his own food show, *State Plate*, found on the INSP cable network and plays concerts around the U.S.

Create. Share. Inspire.

A recipe is more than a combination of ingredients. It's the preamble to the moments we share around the dinner table. For over 160 years, we have been honored to help create the meals that bring us together.

We're the good heat.®

Alagasco

JAMES BEARD AWARDS

BIRMINGHAM'S JAMES BEARD WINNERS & NOMINEES

The James Beard Foundation, a culinary organization dedicated to excellence in the culinary arts, presents its "Oscars" each year honoring elite restaurants and chefs who have reached the pinnacle of their profession. In the past few years, Birmingham restaurants have made a name in the culinary world, in part due to the international recognition these outstanding restaurants and chefs have received as winners and nominees of a James Beard Foundation Award. Leading the way is Highlands Bar and Grill. Since 2009, Chef Frank Stitt, Pardis Stitt, and the Highlands Bar and Grill team have been recognized as one of the most outstanding restaurants in the U.S. by the James Beard Foundation. Birmingham's list of James Beard Award winners and nominees includes:

Chef Frank Stitt, Pardis Stitt | Highlands Bar and Grill
Nominee, Best Chef Southeast 1996, 1998, 1999, 2000
Winner, Best Chef Southeast 2001
Nominee, Cooking from a Chef's Point of View: *Frank Stitt's Southern Table: Recipes and Gracious Traditions from Highlands Bar and Grill* 2005
Nominee, Outstanding Chef 2008
Semifinalist, Outstanding Chef 2009, 2010, 2011
Winner, Who's Who of Food and Beverages in America 2011
Semifinalist, Outstanding Restaurant in America,
Nominee, Outstanding Restaurant in America 2009, 2010, 2011, 2012, 2013, 2014, 2015, 2016, 2017

Chef Dolester Miles | Highlands Bar and Grill, Bottega
Nominee, Outstanding Pastry Chef 2016, 2017
Semifinalist, Outstanding Pastry Chef 2014, 2015

Chef Timothy Hontzas | Johnny's Restaurant
Semifinalist, Best Chef South 2017

Chef Chris Hastings | Hot and Hot Fish Club
Semifinalist, Best Chef South 2009
Nominee, Best Chef South 2007, 2008, 2010, 2011
Winner, Best Chef South 2012

Nick Pihakis | Jim 'n Nick's BBQ Restaurant, Fresh Hospitality Group
Semifinalist, Outstanding Restaurateur 2010, 2011, 2012, 2013, 2014, 2015

Chef Chris and Anna Newsome | Ollie Irene
Semifinalist, Best New Restaurant 2012
Semifinalist, Best Chef South 2015

Chef James Lewis | Bettola
Semifinalist, Best Chef South 2012, 2013

Chef Chris DuPont | Café DuPont
Semifiinalist, Best Chef South 2011

The Bright Star | Jimmy Koikos, Nicky Koikos, Stacey Craig
Winner, America's Classics 2010

James Beard Award nominee Dolester Miles has been a pastry chef at Highlands Bar and Grill and other Frank Stitt restaurants since Highlands opened in 1982.

NEIGHBORHOOD INDEX

ACIPCO/FINLEY
Niki's West, **196**

AVONDALE
Big Spoon Creamery, **204**
Post Office Pies, **108**
Saw's Soul Kitchen, **154**
The Marble Ring, **54**

BESSEMER
The Bright Star, **168**

CAHABA HEIGHTS
Ashley Mac's, **122**
Blackwell's Pub & Eatery, **176**
Satterfield's Restaurant, **180**
The Pita Stop, **88**

CRESTLINE PARK
Saw's Juke Joint, **62**

CRESTLINE VILLAGE
Dyron's Lowcountry, **58, 128**
Miss Dots, **162**
Saw's Juke Joint, **62**
Zoës Kitchen, **124**

DOWNTOWN
Bamboo on 2nd, **78**
Brick & Tin, **64, 142**
Busy Corner Cheese & Provisions, **144**
Century Restaurant & Bar, **94**
John's City Diner, **68, 110**
Revelator Coffee, **140**
Rib-It-Up, **92**
Roots & Revelry, **74**
Sol's Sandwich Shop & Deli, **132**
Ted's Restaurant, **184**
The Collins Bar, **60**
The Louis, **70**
Yo' Mama's Restaurant, **206**
Z's Restaurant, **218**

ENGLISH VILLAGE
Gallery Bar, **66**
Vino, **178**

FOOD TRUCKS
Big Spoon Creamery, **204**
Shindig's Catering & Food Truck, **148**
Snapper Grabber's, **146**

GREEN SPRINGS
The Great Wall, **82**

FOREST PARK
Little Savannah Restaurant and Bar, **72, 170**
Shindig's Catering & Food Truck, **148**
Silvertron Café, **182**

GREYSTONE
Jim 'N Nick's Bar-B-Q, **164**
Steel City Pops, **194**

HOMEWOOD
Dreamcakes Bakery, **208**
Full Moon Bar-B-Que, **200**
Gianmarco's Restaurant, **160**
Holler & Dash, **130**
Homewood Gourmet, **120**
Jim 'N Nick's Bar-B-Q, **164**
Jinsei, **56**
Steel City Pops, **194**
Nabeel's Café & Market, **96, 190**
Zoës Kitchen, **124**

HOOVER
Formosa Hoover Chinese Restaurant, **134**
Full Moon Bar-B-Que, **200**

INVERNESS
Ashley Mac's, **122**
Full Moon Bar-B-Que, **200**
Zoës Kitchen, **124**

IRONDALE
Irondale Café, **118**

LAKEVIEW
Birmingham Breadworks, **202**
Slice Pizza & Brewhouse, **86**
Sky Castle Gastro Lounge, **90**

LEEDS
Rusty's Bar-B-Q, **210**

MOUNTAIN BROOK VILLAGE
Avo Restaurant, **98**
Dram Whiskey Bar, **52**
Brick & Tin, **64, 142**
dg, **188**
Gilchrist Sandwich Shop, **136**
Olexa's, **198**
The Gardens Café, **172**

PEPPER PLACE
OvenBird, **116**
Pie Lab, **216**

RIVERCHASE
Ashley Mac's, **122**
Jim 'N Nick's Bar-B-Q, **164**

SOUTHSIDE
5 Point Public House, **138**
Bottega, **84**
Bottega Café, **104**
Chez Fonfon, **80**
Full Moon Bar-B-Que, **200**
Giuseppe's Café, **186**
Highlands Bar and Grill, **102**
Hot and Hot Fish Club, **112**
Jim 'N Nick's Bar-B-Q, **164**
Ocean, **158**
Taj India, **166**
The Fish Market Southside, **174**
The Pita Stop, **88**

THE SUMMIT
Steel City Pops, **194**
Zoës Kitchen, **124**

TITUSVILLE
Roberts Cuisine, **220**

TRUSSVILLE
Jim 'N Nick's Bar-B-Q, **164**

VESTAVIA HILLS
Iz Café, **212**
Snapper Grabber's Coastal Kitchen, **146**

Map created by Amy Cash | Map locations are not exact, but flags were placed in the general area of each neighborhood.

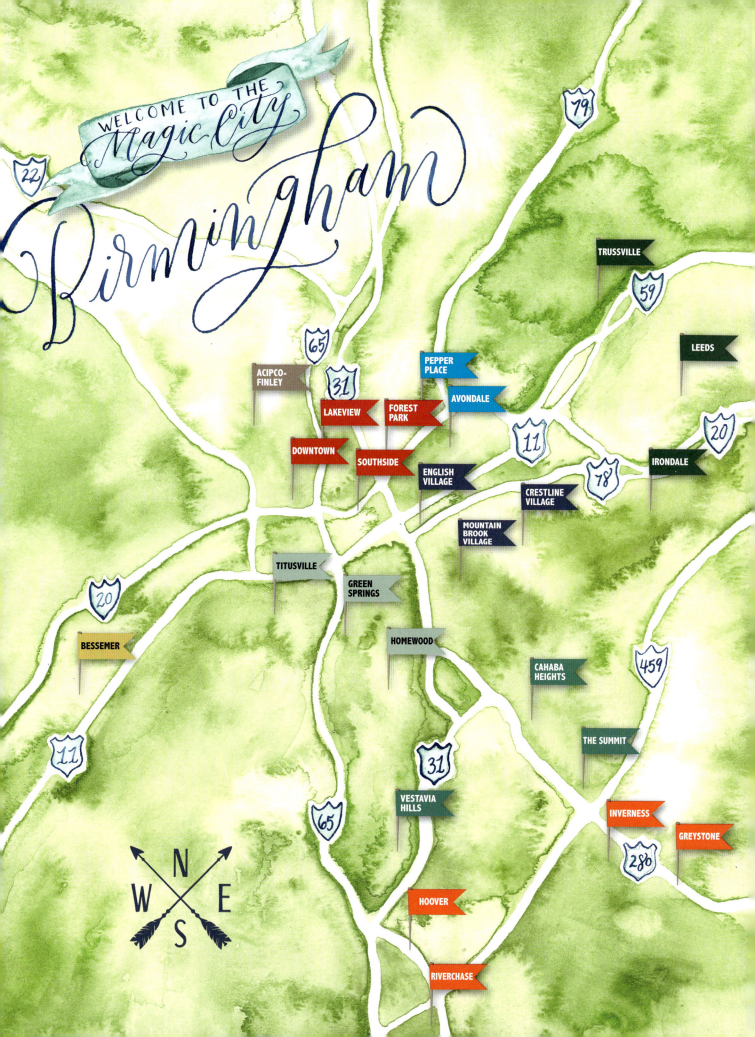

Then & Now

Greek Restaurant Roots 13

Other Distinct Ethnic Influences 16

Magic City Mentors 18

Contemporary Staying Power 21

Fast-Casual Epicenter and Beyond 22

Birmingham
Then & Now

The Story of the Magic City Food Scene

By Chanda Temple

From barbecue and biscuits to pork belly and pizza, Birmingham has captured the hearts and taste buds of its citizens as well as its visitors. Over the past few years, national media outlets, food industry organizations, and online publications have lauded Birmingham for its culinary community, piling on recognition after recognition for food, restaurants, and chefs that impress.

In 2015, national restaurant guide Zagat dubbed Birmingham No. 1 on its "America's Next Hot Food Cities" list. A year later, the guide listed Birmingham as one of "The 26 Hottest Food Cities of 2016." That 2016 distinction landed Birmingham alongside cities such as New York, Chicago, Miami, and San Francisco. In 2017, *The Washington Post* highlighted Birmingham as a travel destination for its "ramped-up food culture" as well as its "revitalized neighborhoods" and different sight-seeing options.

> For Birmingham to become known as a food town is a well-earned distinction...
>
> *- Mayor William A. Bell Sr.*

Gus Koutroulakis ran Pete's Famous Hot Dogs on 2nd Avenue North until he passed away in 2011. His uncle opened the establishment in 1939.

For Birmingham to become known as a food town is a well-earned distinction, Birmingham Mayor William A. Bell Sr. said. "About two years ago, I had the opportunity to speak to writers who wrote about restaurants and things across the country. I found out there were about 200 writers that night, here in Birmingham, writing stories about the food scene here," the mayor said. "The number of restaurants and food establishments that have opened has just exploded here in the city. It's not just the sheer numbers, but it's the quality of the food at all price ranges. And that's what I'm grateful for."

"The downtown area, the Avondale area, and now Woodlawn are starting to get a little attention. And as many places that we

In Birmingham, hot dogs became known for their special meat sauce.

serving up good food. In the early 1900s, Greeks immigrated to Birmingham, bringing with them an approach to food that changed the game on simple dishes of seafood, chicken, steaks, barbecue, and even hot dogs.

Around the turn of the century, downtown Birmingham was a major employment center, filled with office workers looking for a quick bite for lunch. Greek entrepreneurs saw a need and filled

George Sarris' The Fish Market

can continue to add to the food scene, the more people will come here," the mayor said.

For anyone looking to dine with a side of Southern hospitality, Birmingham is the place to be. Diners will find meat-and-threes, fine dining, breweries, hot dog and sandwich shops, food trucks, burgers, barbecue, soul food, hot chicken, tamales, fast casual Japanese, Greek food, and other international fare. But this didn't happen overnight. It's been a phenomenon that's been cooking for quite some time.

GREEK RESTAURANT ROOTS

As far back as the early 20th century, people from various backgrounds put their heart into the city's restaurants. When it came to the Greeks, their hearts beat long and strong for

La Paree on 5th Avenue was originally owned by the Matsos family. It opened in the 1940s and closed in 2003.

MAGIC CITY CRAVINGS   13

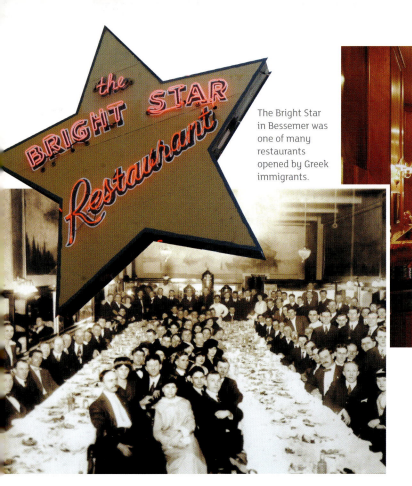

The Bright Star in Bessemer was one of many restaurants opened by Greek immigrants.

options, too. Add Birmingham-based products such as a cold Grapico and a bag of Golden Flake potato chips and lunch on the run was set. Nick Pihakis, the "Nick" of Jim 'N Nick's Bar-B-Q, and his dad would go to Pete's Famous Hotdogs every Saturday, talk to owner Gus Koutroulakis, and eat hot dogs with the signature sauce. It's a tradition he continued with his own son decades later.

Just like the sauce on a Birmingham hot dog pulled people in, it by opening hot dog stands on every block, according to Eric Velasco, a Birmingham freelance writer who has conducted oral history interviews with Birmingham Greek restaurant owners for the Southern Foodways Alliance. It didn't matter if customers were rich or poor—they could afford a hot dog and eat it on the go. Besides the ease and price, they found the meaty sauce on the hot dog tasty. "The sauce is the key. The sauce is what makes the Birmingham dog the Birmingham dog," Velasco said. "That's the common thread here."

Besides the sauce, vintage hot dog condiments in Birmingham consisted of sauerkraut and maybe diced onions, depending on the consumer's preference. Mustard and relish were

> **For a city its size … I think (Birmingham) was really far ahead of its time in regard to the food scene...**
>
> – *John Cassimus, founder of Zoës Kitchen*

The Matsos family was behind early fine-dining establishments Michael's Sirloin Room and La Paree, and later took over Golden Rule Bar-B-Q. Here Jeff Miller, Charles Matsos, and Michael Matsos are pictured in the Golden Rule in Irondale. Although patriarch Michael has passed away, his son Charles continues the legacy with ownership of Golden Rule locations.

The Italian Bruno family opened grocery stores throughout the Southeast, including this one in Homewood in 1965.

Three generations of the Lovoy family ran Lovoy's Italian Restaurant for nearly 60 years. Its original location opened downtown in 1954, and the restaurant closed in 2012.

so did the way the Greeks prepared other foods. But they didn't immediately begin dressing up dishes with their herbs and spices. They found out what people liked—barbecue, meat-and-threes, steak, and seafood—and brought in the oregano, feta cheese, and olive oil later. "It's not like the (110-year-old) Bright Star (in Bessemer) opened with Greek salad or Greek chicken," Velasco said.

The approach worked as Greeks successfully owned and operated a majority of the fine dining establishments in the metro Birmingham area in the 1940s, 1950s, and 1960s. Although popular restaurants such as LaParee, Michael's Sirloin Room, and Rossi's Italian Restaurant, which were owned by Greeks, are now closed, several Greek-owned restaurants from the past still do business today. Some include Niki's West Steak and Seafood Restaurant, The Smokehouse Steak & Seafood Restaurant, Ted's Restaurant, Fife's Restaurant, Demetri's BBQ, and Gus' Hot Dogs, according to Velasco. Present-day favorites such as Jim 'N Nick's Bar-B-Q, Sam's Super Sandwiches, Johnny's Restaurant, Nabeel's Cafe & Market, and the Fish Market are also owned by Greeks.

"For a city its size ... I think [Birmingham] was really far ahead of its time in regard to the food scene. And a lot of it had to do with the ethnic immigrants, like my granddad and other people, that came over," said John Cassimus, founder of Zoës Kitchen, Maki Fresh, Jinsei Sushi, and Miss Dots. His Greek grandfather,

Green Acres Café is one of the African-American-owned restaurants in the 4th Avenue Business District that has been around for decades. Here, owner Greg Gratton is pictured with the café's fried chicken wings.

John Proferis, started the popular John's Restaurant in downtown Birmingham in the 1940s. (Under different ownership now, the restaurant has been known as John's City Diner for the last 13 years.) "Birmingham had such a diverse population back during that time that that was very influential in basically...planting the roots of Birmingham being a great food town," Cassimus said.

Two other Greek-American families with strong and long ties to Birmingham's restaurant history were the Gulases and Jebeles. They owned Jeb's Seven Seas, Louigi's, Gulas' Supper Club, The Elegant, Joe's Ranch House, The Quarterback Drive-In, Andrew's, The Rendezvous, The Blue Note Lounge, The Key Club, Dino's Hot Dogs, Jiffy's Hot Dogs, Johnny's Cafeteria, and Paulson's. Their recipe for homemade Baklava originated in Geraki, Greece, and was handed down to generation after generation in Birmingham.

Food fans of Birmingham are always ready to celebrate the new, but they never fail to cherish the familiar, especially when it's a food festival. Today, the culinary heritage of the city can be seen

Demetri's BBQ is still open in Homewood.

through numerous food festivals throughout the year. The biggest one is the annual Birmingham Greek Festival held in Southside. Other ethnic fare may be found at the St. Elias Lebanese Food and Cultural Festival, Feast of Saint Mark Italian Food Festival, Saint George Middle-Eastern Food Festival, and Friedman Family Foundation Jewish Food Festival.

OTHER DISTINCT ETHNIC INFLUENCES

The Greeks weren't the only immigrants making a mark on the Birmingham food scene. Many Italian families moved to Birmingham to work in the steel business but ended up opening grocery stores to both feed their families and earn an income. Often the stores were run by more than one generation of family members.

Like the Greeks, the Italians' supply met the demand around them. Rosalie Molay, whose grandfather ran Lorino's Grocery, remembers her family's store carrying Italian and Southern foods. "It was a blend of those foods because of what was around you. They adapted themselves to whatever local food there was," she said. "We had pasta every Sunday of my entire life, and we also had fried chicken."

Most notably in this trend, Joseph Bruno, a Sicilian immigrant, opened a small grocery store in downtown Birmingham in the early 1930s. Bruno's Supermarkets would later become a food industry giant with more than 200 stores across the South, according to *The Birmingham News*. The brand was discontinued in 2012. In addition to the grocery business, Italian families opened Lovoy's in 1954 and Ranelli's Deli in 1971. Ranelli's remains open in Southside.

Joy Young Restaurant, which opened in downtown Birmingham in 1919, was popular for its Chinese food, especially its egg rolls and fried chicken. The downtown location closed in the early 1970s.

Jewish entrepreneurs contributed to the building of Birmingham by opening various businesses, including markets. From 1913 to 2009, the Jewish-owned Browdy's delicatessen served steaks and sandwiches along with specials like salmon and eggs and Browdy's Delight (roast beef and coleslaw with Russian dressing on a Kaiser roll). Browdy's moved locations a few times before settling in Mountain Brook Village. Its meat market sold sliced meats and its kosher bakery sold fresh breads and blintzes.

African-American restaurant owners also have deep roots in Birmingham, opening such landmarks as Eagle's Restaurant in North Birmingham in 1951 and Green Acres Cafe in downtown Birmingham in 1958. Both remain in business today.

These restaurants and others provided options for people of color when segregation laws, particularly those of the 1940s, 1950s, and 1960s, barred or limited African Americans' access to various white businesses. A booming Birmingham spot for African Americans at the time was the 4th Avenue Business District, which had a variety of minority-run businesses. Restaurants such as Ma Perkins (also known as Mama Perkins), where patrons could get breakfast for 38 cents and a chicken dinner for 40 cents, and Bob's Savoy (also known as the Little Savoy Café), where T-bone steaks were $1.90, thrived there.

"Everybody who came to town went two places: Bob's Savoy and Ma Perkins. That included (celebrities) James Brown, the Ink Spots, and Billy Eckstine," said longtime Birmingham entrepreneur Jesse Lewis. "It was the location."

Bob's Savoy closed in 1958 after a fire. "Everybody lamented the passing of it. It was a No. 1 first class landmark," said Marjorie White, author of *Downtown Birmingham: Architectural and Historical Walking Tour Guide*. The restaurant was considered the "glamorous heart of the district," where athletes such as Joe Louis, Jackie Robinson, and the Birmingham Black Barons gathered for good food and entertainment while in the segregated South.

Also operating near the 4th Avenue Business District was the African-American-owned Nelson's Brother Café, which opened in the 1940s. Patrons came for the frank sandwiches made with grilled Zeigler's brand sausage on a hamburger bun, the breakfast and burgers, and the egg custard and sweet potato pies made with recipes by founder Daniel Nelson. Daniel died in 1998, but the café remains open today and is run by his son, Jessie Nelson. "The Rev. Martin Luther King Jr. was a visitor here. He would come in here and talk to my daddy," Jessie said.

While additional African-American restaurants such as Rib-It-Up and Z's Restaurant have maintained a presence in downtown

Joy Young interior.

Birmingham for several years, others are just getting started. Eugene's Hot Chicken food truck opened in 2015 in Birmingham to high praise for its Nashville hot chicken. And in 2017, owner Zebbie Carnie opened the company's first brick-and-mortar location in Uptown, generating even more love for his spicy, tempting tenders.

"I'm on a mission to do something great," Zebbie said. "I just wanted to bring something new and something exciting to Birmingham. This is not your mama's fried chicken." Zebbie is proof that if you cook it, they will come. But that hasn't always been the case for Birmingham, which experienced a drop in consumer support for downtown eateries.

In the 1980s, downtown Birmingham restaurants started to stall as chains became the main course and dedicated patrons started to die or move to the suburbs, according to Velasco and al.com. Could Birmingham's food scene rebound? Thankfully, yes.

MAGIC CITY MENTORS

In 1982, Birmingham's food scene started to see new life when a 28-year-old Frank Stitt opened Highlands Bar and Grill. There, he trained young chefs, shared his French techniques, and stressed the use of fresh, southern seasonal produce. His approach took dining to a new level in Birmingham at a time when few high-end restaurants existed in the city. He later opened Italian-inspired Bottega and Bottega Café as well as French bistro Chez Fonfon.

The nation has taken note of Stitt's influence, too. The James Beard Foundation named him Best Chef Southeast in 2001—the same year that *Gourmet* magazine ranked Highlands Bar and Grill No. 5 on its list of top U.S. restaurants. Highlands has also been a James Beard finalist for Outstanding Restaurant in America for 9 consecutive years (2009-2017), bringing acclaim to Stitt and his team.

Highlands pastry chef Dolester "Dol" Miles has been a James Beard Award finalist for Outstanding Pastry Chef, and server Goren Avery was the subject of a 2014 Southern Foodways Alliance documentary, "Red Dog." Both Miles and Avery have worked with Stitt at his restaurants since Highlands opened more than 30 years ago. Stitt works alongside his wife, Pardis, and the couple runs Paradise Farm outside Harpersville. Along the way, he's penned two cookbooks: *Frank Stitt's Southern Table* and *Frank Stitt's Bottega Favorita*.

Chris Hastings, a former sous chef for Stitt, also attracted attention for his food and the way he trained young talent at his Hot and Hot Fish Club. Hastings beat Bobby Flay for the title of Iron Chef on Food Network in 2012, the same year he came home with a Best Chef South award from the James Beard Foundation. Three years after Hot and Hot opened in 1995, it was recognized with the Robert Mondavi Culinary Award of Excellence, and the restaurant has been featured in *The New York Times*, *USA Today*, *Garden & Gun, Southern Living*, and *Food and Wine*. In 2015 Hastings and his wife, Idie, opened OvenBird, a Latin American–inspired wood-fired concept, in what Zagat called "one of the

Brian Somershield, center, co-opened El Barrio after working under Chef Frank Stitt.

Magic City Mentors

Chris Hastings, chef at Hot and Hot Fish Club and OvenBird, is also a Food Network Iron Chef winner.

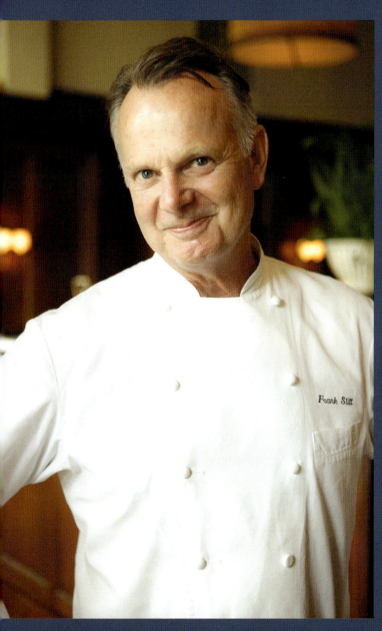

Chef Frank Stitt raised the standard of fine dining in Birmingham not only through his restaurants but through the many chefs in the city he has also trained.

George McMillan III, chef at FoodBar in Cahaba Heights, trained under Hot and Hot Fish Club's Chris Hastings.

Birmingham is known for not only its barbecue and meat-and-threes, but also local restaurants that have become national brands, including Jim 'N Nick's Bar-B-Q. Today, there are 36 Jim 'N Nick's locations across the Southeast. Co-founder Nick Pihakis is pictured on the left.

biggest openings in all of the South." In 2009, the Hastings released the *Hot and Hot Fish Club Cookbook*.

Together, Stitt and Hastings inspired Birmingham restaurateurs to push the envelope in new endeavors, creating meals that mattered in the kitchen and on the table. Brian Somershield of El Barrio, Clifton Holt of Little Savannah, Ryan Champion of Hotbox at Parkside, and Mauricio Papapietro of Brick & Tin all worked under Stitt. Meanwhile, Hastings mentored chefs Daniel Briggs of dg, George McMillan III of FoodBar, and Mac Russell of Shindigs.

Chef George Reis of Ocean, 5 Point Public House Oyster Bar, and the former 26 has also had a hand in providing a training ground for Birmingham restaurant owners. When Brandon Cain and John Hall left Reis to branch out on their own, they made a promise to one another: whoever opened a restaurant first, the other would join him, no matter the location. Cain struck gold first in Birmingham, opening Saw's Soul Kitchen in Avondale in 2012 with Mike Wilson, the owner of the original Saw's BBQ in Homewood. Cain called Hall, who was working in New York at the time, and Hall was in. Eventually, Hall and Cain joined Wilson in opening Post Office Pies next to Saw's Soul Kitchen.

Four years later in 2017, Cain opened Roots & Revelry on the second floor of the 19-story Thomas Jefferson Tower project, a long-vacant building that was once a bustling hotel built in 1929 in downtown Birmingham. Drawing on Reis' influence, Cain did things differently when it came to food. For example, Cain kicked up American cuisine at Roots & Revelry with offerings of Korean hot chicken, a PB&J with homemade cashew butter and pork belly, a patty melt, street tacos, pork inihaw, and even grilled octopus.

"There are opportunities for our chefs in our city. And there are opportunities for entrepreneurs in any form or fashion because it's just now getting turned back on and waking up," Cain said. "It's like any other city. You just have to put a little love and time into it."

John Cassimus, right, built the restaurant his mom, Zoë, left, started, into a national fast-casual brand.

Contemporary Staying Power

Once success happened for them, young chef talent like Cain and Hall didn't leave Birmingham for a bigger or brighter city. They remained in the Magic City to help transform it.

"They stayed here and they planted their roots here, and that's the most exciting thing," Pihakis, who started Jim 'N Nick's with his father, Jim Pihakis, in 1985, said of chefs remaining in Birmingham. "(New restaurants) have reinvested their knowledge and their time into our community, which just makes it stronger."

According to Pihakis, the people help make Birmingham strong. "People make places. And there are so many great places in Birmingham, and getting everyone together is what will help Birmingham to be great."

Also helping to make Birmingham powerful for the palate are the Alabama-based products and fresh produce restaurants are using. Just like the Greeks did years ago, today's chefs are finding new ways to elevate the food experience.

"Here, people will find unique food that they are not going to be able to get anywhere else. Not just unique food, but food with an Alabama connection," said Deontee Gordon, director of business growth for REV Birmingham, an economic development organization. "You can try to get rustic French dishes (elsewhere), but you are not going to get them the way they are done in Birmingham because we are using local ingredients for them."

The Urban Food Project, a program of REV Birmingham, operates a year-round food hub buying, selling, and delivering Alabama-grown produce from 40 small farmers to nearly 35 Birmingham-area restaurants and six stores in food deserts. What started out as Taylor Clark, the director of the Urban Food Project, selling produce from the trunk of her car, has grown into a statewide connection between urban and rural communities, increasing the selling power of the small farmer while creating healthy food access for those who need it most.

Al Hooks Produce, a fourth-generation farm in Shorter, Alabama, has seen various restaurants use its traditional Southern products in new ways. Hooks' purple hull peas are featured on the Soul Pie at Slice Pizza and Brewhouse in Birmingham.

"I think REV is an important bridge for us to use. We are probably in more restaurants because we go through them," said Demetrius Hooks, Al's son and the sales coordinator for Al Hooks Produce. "It's great to see chefs using our foods that we cook one way and use them in another way. I really love coming up to the Birmingham area. It has so much potential for our farm."

Farm-to-table is a concept that is as popular today as it was in the past. Take for example the Ensley Grill in Ensley, which opened in 1930 and closed in 1987. The vegetables that were served at this meat-and-three cafeteria were picked from the 10 acres behind owner Lawrence L. Kilpatrick's house in Minor. They hated to serve anything canned. The farm-fresh vegetables were served with favorites such as standing rib, fried chicken, liver and onions, and butterscotch pie. Similar meat-and-three fare could be found at other notable institutions: Eagle's (which still uses

Niki's West on Finley Avenue is known for its fresh meat and three vegetables.

vegetables from the farmer's market on Finley Avenue), Green Acres on Fourth Avenue North, Ted's Restaurant, and Niki's/Niki's West (longtime supporters of local farmers).

FAST-CASUAL EPICENTER AND BEYOND

As chefs continue to build and support area farmers, Birmingham has become the epicenter of fast-casual restaurant growth, which in turn attracts artisanal chains from beyond its borders.

After several entrepreneurial endeavors of his own, Cassimus took his parents Zoë and Marcus' single Birmingham restaurant, Zoës Kitchen, and built it into a national brand. Over his first 8 years, it grew into 19 units in 5 states, pioneering the fast-casual concept where a customer orders at the counter and their freshly prepared food is brought to their table. Zoës Kitchen went public on the New York Stock Exchange and by 2017, has grown into more than 200 locations in 20 states. Cassimus has started other fast-casual concepts, the Japanese-style Maki Fresh and southern-inspired Miss Dots.

"I did it because I knew the customers were there and they would eat that food," Cassimus said. "And once I learned about Japanese food, I was able to take the Zoës model and use it for Japanese food, and I did Maki Fresh. And Miss Dots was the same model."

Around the same time as the Zoës Kitchen empire was growing, Keith and Amy Richards had a similar idea percolating for a fast-casual concept. While on vacation in Greece in 1997, they noted the warmth and connection they found while eating Mediterranean cuisines in cafes. They wanted to recreate that in Birmingham, where Keith had worked for Frank Stitt's Bottega restaurant for a decade. Influenced by the Greek sauce tzatziki, the couple Americanized it and selected it as the name for their new restaurant. The first Taziki's Mediterranean Café location opened in The Colonnade in 1998. Ten years later, they had 3 locations in Birmingham. Nearly a decade later, Taziki's has grown to more than 70 locations primarily in the Southeast after Keith partnered with Nick Pihakis of Fresh Hospitality Group. Its team is still based in Birmingham, and Keith and Amy's vacation pictures from Greece still deck the walls of the fast-casual eatery.

Other new concepts have selected Birmingham as a test market, too. Cracker Barrel Country Store chose to open the first location of its new fast-casual biscuit concept Holler & Dash in Homewood in 2016. Revelator Coffee started in New Orleans, but moved its headquarters in 2014 to a 10,000-square-foot warehouse in downtown Birmingham to be centrally located in the Southeast. The coffee roaster and retailer entered 6 markets in its first year and now can be found in Chattanooga, Charleston, New Orleans, Nashville, and Atlanta, in addition to Birmingham.

Another restaurant company that has made Alabama home is the New York-based, Mexican street-food inspired Choza Taqueria, one of 13 food stalls housed in the Pizitz Food Hall of the newly-renovated Pizitz Building in downtown Birmingham. Built

> **There are opportunities for our chefs in our city...You just have to put a little love and time into it.**
>
> *– Brandon Cain, Chef/owner, Roots & Revelry*

in 1923, the 9-story former department store building underwent a $60 million dollar renovation project, and the food hall, which is located on the main floor, opened to rave reviews and huge crowds in 2017.

The food hall's popularity continues as visitors can experience food with ethnic diversity: Hawaiian-style poke (a raw fish salad served with seaweed and other vegetables), Asian dumplings, Ethiopian cuisine, Indian dosa, Vietnamese sandwiches, homemade Ramen, chicken and waffles, Mexican ice cream, schwarma, gourmet grilled cheese sandwiches, and flan. Choza Taqueria joins the Busy Cheese Corner, whose owner once

The 1923 Pizitz building reopened in 2017 with a food hall in its bottom level. For decades the building had housed a department store complete with a bakery and restaurants.

worked as a chef at Hot and Hot Fish Club, as well as Revelator Coffee and Alabama Biscuit Co., all at the Pizitz.

"Our owner came here and just fell in love with the place, the project, and the idea," said Charlie Dampf, director of operations for Choza Taqueria, which has 4 locations in Manhattan. Its Birmingham location is the first location outside of New York. "I think it's going to change the downtown area."

Years ago when the building was a department store, a bakery and coffee shop were on the first floor, and a restaurant was on the balcony. The sit-down restaurant, known as the Camellia Room, was open for lunch but closed for dinner. The restaurant opened for dinner during the Christmas season. "We were very famous for our hamburgers before there were a lot of hamburger restaurants," said Michael Pizitz, whose family once owned the building.

Cookies, cakes and pies were sold at the bakery and on the skywalk that led to the parking lot. The wedding and anniversary cakes created by a German pastry chef were bakery fan favorites.

"Back in those days, there were no supermarkets with bakeries. That's why we were so successful in the bakery business," Pizitz said.

Birmingham's love affair with food can be seen in the buzz that continues to build for the city's restaurant scene. In 2017, Facebook CEO Mark Zuckerberg and wife Priscilla Chan visited Hastings' OvenBird restaurant at Pepper Place on their tour of the 50 states. In 2016, Democratic presidential nominee Hillary Clinton took a break from the campaign trail to visit Yo' Mama's and Urban Standard coffee house in downtown Birmingham. In 2010, Oscar winner Sandra Bullock treated her father to a Father's Day dinner at The Bright Star, according to al.com. Opened in 1907 and founded by a Greek immigrant, The Bright Star is Alabama's oldest restaurant still in operation.

Food fans also have love for Birmingham's growing food trucks' community. In 2013, four Birmingham food trucks, including Dreamcakes and Shindigs, made *Deep South* magazine's 2013 list of the "Best Food Trucks in the South." In 2017, there was even talk of an entrepreneur starting a food truck park in downtown Birmingham.

In 2013, Travel Channel food writer and chef Andrew Zimmern taped segments for his *Bizarre Foods America* at several Birmingham eateries, including meat-and-three restaurants Niki's West and Eagle's Restaurant; Jim 'N Nick's Bar-B-Q; and Hot and Hot Fish Club. In 2016, Zimmern returned to Alabama to record segments for *Bizarre Foods: Delicious Destinations*, and stopped by Irondale Café and Bessemer's The Bright Star, among others.

"When you are trying to explore cultures through food, I'm not sure there is a better place to do it than the American South," Zimmern told *The Birmingham News* in 2013. "And when you look at the American South, especially the Southeast, Birmingham is a city with a story [that is] quite remarkable."

Years after Birmingham was founded in 1871, it earned the nickname "The Magic City" because of rapid growth connected to its booming steel industry. Today, a successful steel business has been replaced by other growing industries—and the city's food culture. Recipes from new and old restaurants have left residents and nonresidents taking note, raising a glass, and celebrating the magic on their plate.

Gone But Not Forgotten Favorites

Birmingham food you loved back then and Martie's tips on how to make or find it now

Joy Young
▸▸ Egg Foo Young 26

Marsh Bakery
▸▸ Coconut Cake 28

John's Restaurant
▸▸ Trout Almandine 30

Ireland's
▸▸ Famous Stake An' Biskits 32

Cobb Lane Restaurant
▸▸ She-Crab Soup 34

Pioneer Cafeteria
▸▸ Squash Croquettes 36

Gulas' Restaurant
▸▸ Helen Gulas' Baklava 38

Ed Salem's Drive-In
▸▸ Famous Lemon Icebox Pie 40

Rossi's Italian Restaurant
▸▸ Nick's Famous Greek Snapper 42

Ensley Grill
▸▸ Cinnamon Rolls 44

Grayson's Spinning Wheel
▸▸ Peanut Butter Milkshake 46

JOY YOUNG RESTAURANT

1919-1970s

Joy Young opened in Birmingham in 1919 by a couple reported to be Alabama's first Chinese immigrants. Located across the street from the original Tutwiler Hotel, the restaurant was upscale and elegant with two dining levels plus private dining booths where many couples got engaged to be married. Joy Young was also known at one time for the best fried chicken in Birmingham; a way to embrace their Cantonese roots and Deep South location. They even added homemade yeast rolls to the menu on Sundays to satisfy their clientele.

My own parents went to Joy Young on special occasions with my Aunt Jene and Uncle Ferrell when they could find a babysitter for us kids who were always too young to go to such a fancy fine dining restaurant in downtown Birmingham. When they got home, my mom would tell me about the swanky atmosphere, the egg rolls, and the Egg Foo Young, which was her favorite. As I was scouring her old cookbook for a family recipe, this recipe from the original Joy Young fell out, torn from *The Birmingham News* and worn with time.

-Martie

Tip: If you want an authentic replica of the Joy Young egg rolls today, go to Chop Suey Inn on Green Springs Highway. The owners are relatives of the family who owned Joy Young and claim to have the restaurant's original recipes. I tested them out on my father, and he agrees that the egg rolls, Egg Foo Young, and other dishes are exactly like the ones he remembers from Joy Young. Many other Birmingham diners feel the same way; Chop Suey Inn has a loyal following of former Joy Young customers. The atmosphere isn't as refined as the original Joy Young, but the prices more than make up for that.

GONE BUT NOT FORGOTTEN FAVORITES

EGG FOO YOUNG à la JOY YOUNG

Yield: Serves 6

INGREDIENTS

Vegetable oil

2 celery ribs, *cut diagonally into 1/4-inch slices*

1 small white onion, *halved lengthwise and cut into 1/4-inch strips*

1 green bell pepper, *cut into 1/4-inch strips, then halved*

1 cup bok choy, *cut into 1/4-inch slices (Keep leaves separate.)*

1 cup mushrooms, *cut into 1/4-inch slices*

1 cup snow peas, *cut diagonally into 1/4-inch slices*

1 (5-ounce) can sliced water chestnuts, *drained*

1 (5-ounce) can sliced bamboo shoots, *drained (You can substitute 1 large can chop suey vegetables.)*

4 large eggs, *beaten*

1 (10-ounce) package frozen, cooked shrimp *(You can substitute cooked chicken.)*

2 teaspoons chicken-flavored instant bouillon

Hot cooked rice

Foo Young Sauce:

1 1/2 cups chicken broth

2 tablespoons soy sauce

2 tablespoons cornstarch

1/2 cup water

Salt and pepper to taste

DIRECTIONS:

Heat a very small amount of oil in a hot pan or wok. Add the dense vegetables first: celery, onion, green pepper, and the bulb of the bok choy; sauté about 2 minutes or until tender. Add the mushrooms, snow peas, and the leaves from the bok choy and sauté for 2 minutes more. Add the water chestnuts and bamboo shoots and set aside to cool.

Combine eggs, cooled vegetables, shrimp, and bouillon and let sit for 10 minutes. Mix well.

Heat a small amount of vegetable oil in a large skillet. Spoon 1/4 cup of the mixture into the hot oil, shaping it into a 3-inch circle using a spatula much like you would a pancake. Cook until browned, and then flip and brown the other side. Keep warm on a plate in the oven until all the mixture is used. Add additional oil between batches as needed.

For the Foo Young Sauce: Add the chicken broth to a medium saucepan over low heat. In a bowl or cup, mix the soy sauce and cornstarch together until dissolved, and then whisk into the chicken broth, a little at a time. Bring to a boil and reduce heat to low, stirring constantly until thickened. Add salt and pepper to taste. Remove from heat and keep warm.

Serve the warm pancakes over hot rice and top with Foo Young Sauce.

MARSH BAKERY

1932 – 2006

Marsh Bakery was founded in 1929 by brothers Lloyd and Gail Marsh. Using a small oven in the basement, they made cakes and sold them door to door during the Great Depression as a way to make extra money. They found a following of loyal customers and were able to buy a panel truck for their deliveries. The brothers incorporated in 1932 and opened a bakery in the tiny section of East Lake, once called Floral Park. In the mid '30s, the company moved to the west side of Birmingham. Then, in 1967 they moved into an old Frostop Root Beer location in west Birmingham where they turned the giant Frostop mug sign in front of the building into the iconic 3-D birthday cake sign that Birmingham residents remember well.

Many people have fond memories of Marsh Bakery, usually tied to a holiday or special birthday celebration. Stories about their cakes, rolls, breads, and sandwiches can be found in nostalgic social media posts. When we asked social media about favorite dishes from places that have closed, Marsh Bakery topped the list, with a tie between its birthday cake and its unforgettable coconut cake. For months, I tried to locate the actual family recipe and received several versions from former employees and friends of the bakery. The problem was that one recipe featured a white cake, and the other a golden cake.

Using those recipes as my guide, I recreated the Marsh's recipe to the best of my memory. The bakery still has legions of admirers who claim there will never be another coconut cake as good as the ones from Marsh. If you make this recipe, I hope it brings back memories of the holidays and occasions you celebrated with a Marsh's cake.

- *Martie*

> **Tip:** Today, my favorite coconut cake is Chef Frank Stitt's famous Coconut Pecan Cake at Chez Fonfon and Bottega Café made by James Beard-nominated pastry chef Dolester Miles. The cake has cream of coconut in it, which makes it incredibly moist and rich, and toasted coconut on the top and sides. They serve it in a pool of luscious Crème Anglaise. Be sure to try it!

Coconut Cake à la Marsh Bakery

GONE BUT NOT FORGOTTEN FAVORITES

COCONUT CAKE
à la MARSH BAKERY

Yield: 1 (9-inch) layer cake or approximately 12-14 slices

INGREDIENTS

Cake:

5 egg whites, *at room temperature*

1/2 cup whole milk, *at room temperature*

1 teaspoon coconut extract

1 teaspoon vanilla extract

3 cups cake flour, *sifted, plus more to flour pans*

2 cups granulated sugar

3 1/2 teaspoons baking powder

1/4 teaspoon salt

1 cup (2 sticks) unsalted butter, *at room temperature*

1 cup unsweetened coconut milk

Icing:

3 large egg whites

1/3 cup water

1 3/4 cups granulated sugar

1/2 teaspoon cream of tartar

Pinch salt

1 teaspoon vanilla extract

1/2 teaspoon coconut extract

1 1/2 cups sweetened shredded coconut for garnish

DIRECTIONS:

For the cake: Preheat oven to 350° Fahrenheit. Grease and flour 2 (9-inch) cake pans.

In a small bowl, whisk together the egg whites, milk, and extracts. Set aside. In the bowl of a stand mixer fitted with the paddle attachment, combine the flour, sugar, baking powder, and salt. Add the butter and coconut milk, and combine on low speed until moistened. Increase the speed to medium and beat until light and fluffy, about 2 minutes.

Add the egg white mixture in 3 additions, scraping down the sides of the bowl and mixing just long enough to incorporate between additions.

Divide the batter between the prepared pans and bake for 35-40 minutes or until a toothpick inserted into the center comes out clean. Allow the cakes to cool in their pans for 10 minutes before removing to cool on a wire baker's rack. Allow to cool completely before frosting. Use a serrated knife or dental floss to slice the cakes in half to create 4 layers.

For the icing: Add 4 cups water to a saucepan and bring to a boil. Reduce the heat to medium. (It is a good idea to make sure the water does not touch the bowl before you combine your ingredients, so check it now. If it does touch, pour out some of the water and bring it back to a simmer before proceeding. You will need to beat the icing for 7 minutes, so make sure you're ready because you can't stop once you begin.) Use a large bowl as the icing will almost triple in volume.

Place the egg whites, water, sugar, cream of tartar, and salt into a heatproof bowl and place the bowl over the simmering water. Beat for 1 minute on low using a hand mixer. Increase the speed and beat on high for 5 minutes. Remove the bowl from heat but continue beating for 1 additional minute as you add in the extracts. Allow the frosting to cool slightly before spreading onto the cake layers.

Place your cake plate on a baking sheet or large piece of parchment paper to catch the excess coconut as it falls. Working quickly, spread icing across bottom layer of cake. Sprinkle with a portion of the coconut. Repeat for the additional layers of cake, and then frost the top and sides. Use your hand to gently press the coconut onto the sides of the cake to help it stick.

You will achieve the best results if you refrigerate the cake for at least 1 hour before slicing; it is best to remove it from the refrigerator 15 minutes prior to slicing.

Trout Almandine à la John's

(Above) John Proferis (Below) Zoe and John Cassimus

JOHN'S RESTAURANT

1944-2003

Many Birmingham restaurants have served a version of Trout Almandine, but it is thought to have first become popular at the original John's Restaurant, which was then located at 214 21st Street North. The dish at John's may or may not have always been trout; the dish was created to use the leftover "fat" part of the fish of the day that was pan fried and topped with roasted almonds.

Each chef I interviewed for this recipe had a different spin on it. One thing they all agreed upon was to take time to melt the butter properly. Browned butter is the key to the flavor in the dish. Another chef note is to watch the almonds carefully because they will burn in the blink of an eye. Once you can smell them, they are done.

John Proferis, the late father of Zoës Kitchen founder Zoë Cassimus, opened John's in 1944, and it quickly became known for its meat-and-three during lunch hours and their fresh seafood. On Sundays, guests would hurry to John's from church for lunch, so they could be assured an order of John's famous pot roast and accompanying basket of corn sticks. (Today you can find a similar pot roast at Johnny's Restaurant in Homewood.)

Nick Pihakis of Jim 'n Nick's Bar-B-Q and Fresh Hospitality Group fondly remembers the Sunday rush at John's: "It was essential to arrive before noon on Sundays, or you'd miss out on the pot roast." Proferis' grandson, John Cassimus of Zoës Kitchen and University of Alabama fame, remembers the giant cinnamon rolls that were rolled out in the kitchen daily: "As a kid, that was a big part of going to my grandfather's restaurant."

Another John's recipe with a big following is John's slaw; the finely shredded cabbage was generously doused with a house-made French dressing. You can buy the John's Famous Angel Hair Slaw & Salad Dressing in grocery stores today.

- *Martie*

TROUT ALMANDINE
à la JOHN'S

Yield: Serves 4-6

INGREDIENTS

1 cup all-purpose flour

1 teaspoon Greek seasoning *(Greek oregano, thyme, and rosemary)*

1 cup buttermilk or whole milk

6-8 trout filets, skin removed *(You can substitute red snapper.)*

Salt and pepper to taste

1 stick (1/2 cup) unsalted butter, *divided*

1/2 cup sliced almonds

Juice of 1 lemon, plus a lemon wedge for garnish

DIRECTIONS:

On a plate or shallow dish, mix the flour and the Greek seasoning together. Put the milk in a separate shallow bowl.

Season the fish with salt and pepper. Dip it into the milk and shake to remove the excess. Dredge in the seasoned flour and again shake to remove the excess.

Melt half the butter (4 tablespoons) in a large sauté pan on medium-high heat. Cook the fish filets until they are golden brown. Flip and cook the other side and remove to a warm platter in the oven. Set aside.

Add the remaining butter to the same pan. Brown the butter slowly by swirling the pan over the heat until the butter smells nutty and turns light brown. This is a slow process; cooking the butter too fast will usually result in burned butter. The butter will foam during cooking, which is what you want. Once the butter begins to turn pale brown, lower the heat and add the almonds, continuing to swirl the pan while stirring occasionally. Once the almonds are brown, add the lemon juice and season with salt and pepper to taste. Spoon the hot butter and almonds over the fish and serve while the sauce is still foamy.

Ireland's Famous Stake an' Biskits

IRELAND'S

1942 – 1982

Ireland's was the first chain of restaurants to originate in Birmingham and move into other cities. There were two Birmingham locations before the company expanded north to Huntsville, Nashville, Memphis, and Knoxville. The restaurant closed in the early 1980s, but people still fondly remember the Stake an' Biskits. Former employees say that the dish originated as a savvy restaurateur's way to use scraps of leftover filet from their Tuesday night Filet Special. The special featured a filet, salad, and potato for a whopping $5.99 back in the mid-'70s. Their Killarney Fudge Pie, served warm with a scoop of ice cream, was another highly requested recipe.

 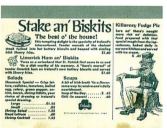

You may certainly use your own biscuit recipe or frozen biscuits in lieu of making these biscuits from scratch to save a bit of time, but make sure you butter the hot biscuits with a huge pat of real salted butter before adding the hot steak. That is what makes the "gravy" sauce.

> **TIP:** Ireland's Stake an' Biskits were always served with a huge pile of well-salted shoestring French fries called "skerry fries" on top. Today, you can order a very similar version of this classic Ireland's recipe at Dram in Mountain Brook Village.

GONE BUT NOT FORGOTTEN FAVORITES

IRELAND'S FAMOUS STAKE an' BISKITS
(Steak and Biscuits)

Yield: 12 biscuits

INGREDIENTS

Steak:

3 tablespoons vegetable oil, *divided*

2 cloves garlic, *minced*

1 teaspoon kosher salt, *divided*

1/2 teaspoon ground pepper, *divided*

1 (2-pound) beef tenderloin, *sliced into 1/4-1/2-inch medallions*

Biscuits:

3 cups all-purpose flour, *plus more for dusting*

2 teaspoons baking powder

1/2 teaspoon baking soda

3/4 teaspoon salt

3/4 cup shortening

1 1/4 cups whole buttermilk

1 stick (1/2 cup) salted butter, *at room temperature*

DIRECTIONS:

For the steak: In a glass bowl or plastic zip-top bag, add 2 tablespoons oil, garlic, 1/2 teaspoon salt, and 1/4 teaspoon pepper and whisk or shake well to make the marinade. Add the beef. Marinate in the refrigerator for at least 8 hours and up to 24 hours.

For the biscuits: Preheat oven to 425° Fahrenheit. Remove the beef from the refrigerator and allow to come to room temperature.

In a large bowl, whisk the flour, baking powder, baking soda, and salt together. Cut in the shortening using a pastry cutter or two forks until incorporated. Make a well in the center of the flour. Pour in the buttermilk. Stir to combine, just until it comes together; the dough should be shaggy and slightly wet.

Lightly dust the counter with flour. Turn the dough out. Dust the top and your hands. Fold the dough over onto itself, dusting and kneading for approximately 5 minutes. Dust a rolling pin; roll the dough out about 1/3-inch thick.

Using a 2-inch biscuit cutter, press it into flour and then press straight down into the dough. Place the biscuits on the baking sheet, making sure they are slightly touching. Bake on the lower shelf for 10 minutes. Rotate the pan and bake 3-4 more minutes or until golden brown.

While the biscuits are baking, begin to heat a large cast iron skillet or grill pan. You may wipe a bit of oil onto the pan, but you won't use oil to cook the beef; it is meant to be seared. The pan is meant to be extremely hot but not smoking when you sear the meat.

Remove the beef from the marinade. Shake off the excess marinade, but do not blot. Salt and pepper both sides and sear for 1 minute per side. Remove to a heated plate until the biscuits are done.

To serve, split the hot biscuit, add a pat of the butter to the inside of each biscuit, and put a slice of the hot tenderloin inside. The biscuits are meant to be served with the butter dripping from them, making a kind of sauce when combined with the juices from the hot tenderloin.

Cobb Lane She-Crab Soup

COBB LANE RESTAURANT

1948-2009

Virginia Cobb started serving tea sandwiches as refreshments at her dress shop in 1948. The restaurant closed in 2009 after 61 years in business.

As the popularity of her food grew, Mrs. Cobb started serving lunch, featuring Southern favorites like Chicken Divan, Chicken Supreme, and warm homemade yeast rolls served with every meal. She also added courtyard dining, which was extremely popular for bridesmaid luncheons, baby showers, and other celebrations. It was such a popular spot that the city named the brick alley in her honor, calling it Cobb Lane. Following Virginia Cobb's death in 1987, Mikki Bond took over the restaurant and published a cookbook of Mrs. Cobb's recipes. After several changes of ownership, the restaurant closed for good in 2009. Fans of the restaurant still talk about its famous She-Crab Soup and signature Chocolate Roulage.

It is reported that Julia Child once said Cobb Lane's She-Crab Soup was the best she'd ever eaten. Here is a version of Mrs. Cobb's celebrated recipe.

> **TIP:** When she-crabs are in season (typically from late April until the first cold snap), you can occasionally find a rich and delicate She-Crab Soup at Dyron's Lowcountry (found on pages 58 and 128) in Crestline Village. Make sure to call or check its website to confirm availability.

GONE BUT NOT FORGOTTEN FAVORITES

COBB LANE SHE-CRAB SOUP

Yield: Serves 12-16, depending on portion size

INGREDIENTS

1/3 cup yellow onion, *diced*

1 cup celery, *diced*

2 tablespoons unsalted butter

2 quarts fresh chicken stock *(You may use canned.)*

1 cup fresh button mushrooms, *chopped*

1 tablespoon dried basil

1 tablespoon dried oregano

1 tablespoon dried chives

1 teaspoon dried thyme

3 bay leaves

2 cups cooked rice

1 teaspoon Worcestershire sauce

3 cups homemade cream of mushroom soup *(You may use canned.)*

2 quarts whipping cream

1 quart whole milk

3 pints fresh lump blue crabmeat *(Remove shells, but do not wash.)*

1 tablespoon lemon pepper seasoning

1 teaspoon Tabasco sauce

Salt and pepper to taste

Sherry for finishing

DIRECTIONS:

Sauté onion and celery in the butter until onions are transparent but not brown. Add chicken stock, mushrooms, basil, oregano, chives, thyme, bay leaves, and rice. Bring to a boil then reduce heat to low and simmer for 20 minutes.

Add the Worcestershire, soup, whipping cream, milk, crabmeat, lemon pepper seasoning, and Tabasco. Cook 1 hour more in a double boiler over simmering water. Check seasoning, adding more salt, pepper, Tabasco, or Worcestershire as desired.

Finish with a dollop of sherry or serve it on the side as they did at Cobb Lane.

Pioneer's Squash Croquettes

PIONEER CAFETERIA

1959-2004

The Pioneer Cafeteria was started in 1959 on the eastern side of Birmingham on Parkway East as a steam table buffet restaurant. Owned by Marvin Ratcliff, it became an area fixture known for favorites like lasagna, country fried steak, fresh vegetables, homemade yeast rolls, and desserts. Ratcliff later opened two other locations and a private dining club in the back of the Parkway East location. At the Pioneer Supper Club, members enjoyed dining and dancing with waiter service and a bar, something not offered in the cafeteria.

I fondly remember going to the Pioneer after church on Sundays. I'd get stuck at the desserts, trying to decide between the different mile-high pies and the various, colorful Jell-O offerings. My parents took me to the Supper Club for my 13th birthday, and I was allowed to order a Shirley Temple faux cocktail that came in a fancy glass with a paper umbrella and a Maraschino cherry garnish. Boy, did I think I was grown up! Many people who remember the Pioneer requested its famous squash croquettes recipe. We were lucky to track down the original recipe from Linda Simms; her husband, Eddie, bought the restaurant from Ratcliff in 1988.
- Martie

TIP: If you don't want to cook, you will find a very similar version of the Pioneer's squash croquettes at Fife's Restaurant located in downtown Birmingham at 2321 4th Avenue North. The recipe for Fife's Squash Croquettes was featured in *Birmingham's Best Bites*.

GONE BUT NOT FORGOTTEN FAVORITES

PIONEER'S SQUASH CROQUETTES

Yield: Serves 12

INGREDIENTS

2 pounds choice yellow squash *(about 6 medium squash)*

1 cup yellow onion, *minced*

1 stick margarine

1 cup butter

4 eggs, well beaten

2 cups white bread crumbs, *plus more for rolling*

1 cup cornbread crumbs

1/2 tablespoon salt

1/2 teaspoon black pepper

1/2 teaspoon granulated sugar

1/2 cup vegetable oil, for frying

DIRECTIONS:

Cut squash into slices about 1/2-inch thick. Add to a pot of water, making sure to just cover the squash. Bring to a boil, reduce heat, and then cook until fork tender. Allow to drain thoroughly for 3 hours in the refrigerator.

Sauté onions in a saucepan in margarine until brown. Cool.

Place drained squash in a large bowl. Add the onions and all remaining ingredients except the oil, mixing well.

Shape croquettes using a No. 12 size ice cream scoop and roll in the extra white bread crumbs.

Deep fry in oil heated to 350° Fahrenheit until golden brown. Drain on paper towels.

Helen Gulas' Baklava

GULAS' RESTAURANT and LOUNGE, DINO'S HOT DOGS and GULAS' SUPPER CLUB

1950s - present

There have been several popular Gulas and Jebeles family-owned restaurants in Birmingham over the past 100 years. Gulas' Restaurant and Lounge and Gulas' Supper Club were fine dining restaurants, known for charbroiled steaks, prime rib, trout almandine, homemade desserts, and live entertainment. Additionally, Jeb's Seven Seas, Louigi's, The Elegant, Joe's Ranch House, The Quarterback Drive-in, Andrew's BBQ, The Rendezvous, The Blue Note Lounge, The Key Club, Dino's Hot Dogs, Jiffy's Hot Dogs, Johnny's Cafeteria, and Paulson's were all popular area restaurants owned by these families.

Most of the Gulas restaurants sold baklava, but it was synonymous with Dino's Hot Dogs. I especially remember the Huffman location. We would stop in there after ball practice, and Mr. Gulas (Aleck Gulas) would always make sure you took home some baklava.

When I asked my Birmingham Facebook friends for their favorite "days gone by" dishes, I got a recipe and this great story from my friend Bunny Tatarek: "Helen Gulas was a patient at the hospital where I was working as her nurse. I knew of the family from the Gulas restaurants, and we got to know each other a bit during her stay. I always loved the baklava and asked her for the recipe. She wrote it out for me, even drawing a diagram which shows how to slice the baklava. I've saved it all these years, and it is without a doubt the best baklava ever."

Bunny shared Mrs. Gulas' original handwritten recipe with me for the book. I showed it to Ike Gulas, who confirmed to me that it is his mother's handwriting and the family's original baklava recipe that has been handed down for generations. According to Ike, the recipe originated in the village of Geraki in the south of Greece, part of the region which made up Sparta. It was handed down from Ike's grandmother Katherine Jebeles to his mother, Helen Jebeles Gulas. Helen later taught Ike's wife, Fanoula, how to make it.

- *Martie*

Tip: For those of you who don't cook, you're in luck! Fanoula's company, The Greek Kouzina, sells the Gulas family baklava and other homemade Greek pastries at several locations and food festivals around Birmingham.

GONE BUT NOT FORGOTTEN FAVORITES

HELEN GULAS' BAKLAVA

Yield: Approximately 32 pieces

INGREDIENTS

6 cups pecans, *finely chopped*

3 cups granulated sugar, *divided*

2 teaspoons ground cinnamon

1 pound phyllo dough *(Find it in the freezer section of most grocery stores.)*

2 cups (4 sticks) unsalted butter

1 1/4 cups water

Juice from 1/2 a lemon

1/2 cup honey

DIRECTIONS:

Preheat oven to 325° Fahrenheit.

Mix the chopped pecans with 1/2 cup sugar and cinnamon. Set aside.

Reserve 6 sheets of phyllo for the top. Set these aside covered with a clean, damp tea towel so they do not dry out.

Melt the butter. Using a soft pastry brush, butter the bottom and sides of a 13x9-inch baking pan. Separately add 4 sheets of phyllo to the bottom of the pan, brushing each layer of phyllo with butter before adding the next. Work quickly so the phyllo does not dry out. To prevent the edges from cracking, lightly brush the edges first and work into the center. Sprinkle with 1/3 of the nut mixture. Repeat this process 2 more times.

Separately, add the final 6 sheets of phyllo to the top, again brushing each sheet with butter. Sprinkle the top layer with water, and trim the edges of the dough if necessary. Score the top of the baklava into diamond shapes. (Mrs. Gulas' diagram indicates 3-4 vertical rows with diagonal scores running the length of each row.)

Bake at 325° for 1 hour. While the baklava is baking, make the syrup, allowing it to cool before use.

For the syrup: Add 2 1/2 cups sugar, water, and lemon juice to a saucepan. Bring to a boil, reduce the heat, and cook for 15 minutes or until thickened. Remove from heat and allow to cool. Stir in the honey.

When the baklava is done, remove from the oven, and pour the syrup over the baklava while it is still hot.

Allow to set for at least 2-3 hours before cutting.

Ed Salem's Famous Lemon Icebox Pie

ED SALEM'S DRIVE-IN

1953-1983

University of Alabama All-American football great Ed Salem created one of the first fast-food chains of the time when he opened his iconic Ed Salem's Drive-In restaurants. The first location opened in 1953 at 10th Avenue and 26th Street North and featured burgers, fries covered in gravy, ice cream sodas, and its famous Lemon Icebox Pie. This wasn't just a teen hangout. Even football greats Paul "Bear" Bryant and Joe Namath were regulars. A second location opened soon afterward at 3201 3rd Avenue South.

In 1958, the Southside location was purchased at the site that had housed Eli's Sky Castle Drive In situated in the heart of the Lakeview District. A glass "tower" had been built above the restaurant as a broadcast booth for WSGN radio station. DJs would take requests and spin hits, and guests would drive up, order from carhops on roller skates, and place a request with the DJ via a telephone handset mounted to the exterior wall.

Today, in that same Lakeview location, Birmingham's Bajalieh brothers, owners of Slice Pizza & Brewhouse, and Sol's Sandwich Shop & Deli, pay homage to Ed Salem and the early days of Birmingham radio with their gastropub concept restaurant called Sky Castle.

Tip: If you want to try the real thing, Ed Salem's son, Wayne Salem, is making his father's famous Lemon Icebox Pie at his Homewood restaurant, Salem's Diner, 2913 18th Street South. While you are there, try his Philly Cheesesteak Sandwich, which television host Craig Ferguson deemed the best he has ever tasted! - *Martie*

GONE BUT NOT FORGOTTEN FAVORITES

ED SALEM'S FAMOUS LEMON ICEBOX PIE

Yield: 1 (9-inch) pie

INGREDIENTS

- 8-10 lemons, freshly squeezed
- 2 (14-ounce) cans sweetened condensed milk
- 2 eggs, beaten well
- 1 (9-ounce) graham cracker pie crust *(Or you can make your own in a 9-inch pie pan.)*
- Whipped topping

DIRECTIONS:

Preheat oven to 350° Fahrenheit.

Squeeze the lemons and whisk the juice into the eggs and condensed milk. Pour the mixture into the pie crust. Bake for 10-12 minutes.

Remove and let cool on a baker's rack. Top with your favorite whipped topping or make your own using heavy cream and Confectioners sugar.

Notes

Nick's Famous Greek Snapper

ROSSI'S ITALIAN RESTAURANT

Rossi's was a Birmingham institution for many years; it was located upstairs above the original Michael's Sirloin Room on what was known as "The Strip" on 20th Street and 5th Avenue South. Veal Piccata and Veal Saltimbocca were local favorites, along with many traditional Italian specialties.

Jim 'N Nick's founder Nick Pihakis has fond memories of Rossi's; he spent part of his early career in the restaurant business working there. One dish he loves to prepare is Greek Snapper, a recipe inspired from his days working at Rossi's. Nick says his family always makes this Greek Snapper recipe when they are together at the beach; it is a family tradition. It is also a quick and delicious way to cook fish at home. Nick suggests using two dishes so that you do not overcook the fish since the onions take longer to cook than the fish.

> **Tip:** When at home in Birmingham, Nick shops at Sexton's in Cahaba Heights for fresh snapper. - *Martie*

GONE BUT NOT FORGOTTEN FAVORITES

NICK'S FAMOUS GREEK SNAPPER INSPIRED by ROSSI'S

Yield: Serves 4

INGREDIENTS

1 yellow onion, sliced 1/4-inch thick

1-2 large tomatoes, *sliced 1/2-inch thick*

1/2 cup white wine

1/2 cup lemon juice

Salt and pepper to taste

1 stick unsalted butter, at room temperature, *divided*

4 (10-ounce) fresh Gulf snapper fillets

2 tablespoons fresh basil chiffonade for garnish

DIRECTIONS:

Preheat oven to 350° Fahrenheit.

Layer the onions on the bottom of a heatproof dish or pan. Add a layer of tomatoes on top of the onions.

In a bowl, whisk together white wine and lemon juice. Pour half of the mixture over the onions and tomatoes. Salt and pepper generously. Dot the top with half of the butter. Bake uncovered at 350° for 25-30 minutes or until onions are extremely tender.

After the onions have cooked for 20 minutes, place the fish in a separate dish. Pour the remaining lemon-wine mixture over the top. Salt and pepper generously. Dot the top with the remaining butter. Bake at 350° for 10-15 minutes or until done. Time will be determined by the thickness of the fish. (Calculate approximately 15 minutes of cooking time per 1-inch thickness of fish at the thickest part.)

Once the fish is done, remove both dishes from the oven. Add the basil to the onions. Combine the cooking liquid from both dishes and whisk together.

To plate: Place one fillet on the plate and top with the onions and tomato. Ladle some of the cooking liquid over the top and serve.

Cinnamon Rolls à la Ensley Grill

ENSLEY GRILL
(Also known as
The Ensley Grill Cafeteria)

1930-1987

Lawrence L. Kilpatrick, known by friends and family as "LL," was the owner of the Ensley Grill. According to his family, he was born in New Orleans to Lars and Nora Lee Kilpatrick, who immigrated to the United States from Ireland. The family moved to Birmingham when Lars came to the booming Steel City to look for work. Lawrence started the restaurant in November 1930 as a street stand on 19th Street in Ensley. He soon built a following and eventually rented the building he'd been standing in front of during those early years. His parents were his first employees.

A true pioneer in farm to table cooking, Lawrence grew some of his own vegetables on 10 acres of land he leased behind the family home in Minor. He hated to serve anything that was not fresh. Nathan Madison the manager of the grill would often man the carving station during the restaurant's evening rush. As someone came down the line, he would sing out, "Serve you, please?"

Social media posts from former patrons longingly recall many of the dishes the restaurant was known for: Standing Rib Roast, Fried Chicken, Liver and Onions, Butterscotch Pie, and especially the homemade breads. The restaurant's homemade cinnamon rolls and onion rolls were famous in their time; many recall them being "as big as your fist." We got dozens of requests for the recipe and a trip down memory lane.

On April 16, 1986, an after-hours robbery resulted in the murder of Mr. Madison. The family and Ensley community never got over the tragedy, and the restaurant closed in 1989. Lawrence is fondly remembered by his customers who still crave his recipes almost 30 years later.

Since we were not able to source the exact Ensley Grill recipe for Cinnamon Rolls, I tested several until I came up with one that resembles those fist-sized rolls.
— *Martie*

> **Tip:** Today my favorite cinnamon rolls are found at Niki's West; they are on the menu during breakfast and after 4 p.m. when you order from the dinner menu. If you don't want to bake, make a beeline to Finley Avenue and get one while they are warm. You can order dozens to-go for your next office party, holiday breakfast, or brunch.

GONE BUT NOT FORGOTTEN FAVORITES

CINNAMON ROLLS à la ENSLEY GRILL

Yield: 3 dozen large Ensley Grill-size cinnamon rolls or about 50 regular-size cinnamon rolls

INGREDIENTS

Cinnamon Rolls:

2 ounces (8 (1/4-ounce) packages) active dry yeast

1/2 cup plus 4 tablespoons granulated sugar, *divided*

2 cups lukewarm water, *divided*

2 cups milk

1/2 cup plus 2 tablespoons shortening

2 tablespoons salt

2 eggs, beaten

10 1/2 cups all-purpose flour plus more for dusting

1/4 cup unsalted butter plus more for the pans and bowls, *at room temperature*

1 cup dark brown sugar

2 tablespoons ground cinnamon

Icing:

1/2 cup unsalted butter, *at room temperature*

8 cups Confectioners sugar

1/4 teaspoon salt

1 1/2 teaspoons vanilla extract

8-10 tablespoons milk

DIRECTIONS:

For the cinnamon rolls: Butter several large baking pans or line them with parchment paper.

Dissolve yeast and 2 tablespoons of sugar in 1/2 cup lukewarm water; stir until completely dissolved. Add 1 1/2 cups more lukewarm water and set aside to bloom.

In a medium saucepan, scald milk by heating it over medium-high heat until tiny bubbles begin to form around the sides of the pan. Do not allow it to boil. Remove from heat and let it cool slightly. Add shortening, remaining 1/2 cup plus 2 tablespoons granulated sugar, and salt. Stir until dissolved. Cool.

Add the 2 beaten eggs to the milk mixture once it has cooled. Combine the milk mixture and the yeast mixture and gradually stir in the flour.

Turn the dough out onto a floured board and knead until the dough is smooth.

Put dough into greased bowl and cover with a tea towel. Place in warm spot for 1 hour. After 1 hour, punch the dough down in the bowl and let stand for another 45 minutes.

Flour the workspace and roll out the dough in a rectangle. Brush the dough with 1/4 cup butter and sprinkle with the brown sugar and cinnamon.

Roll the dough up; roll from the long side of the rectangle so you have a long, thin shape. Slice in 1 1/2-inch pieces and flatten each slice slightly with the palm of your hand. Place the slices on buttered pans or cookie sheets.

Preheat oven to 350° Fahrenheit. Let stand in warm place for 45 minutes, and then bake 25 minutes. Remove from oven and immediately turn out onto a wire baking rack with parchment paper underneath. After the rolls are cooled for about 7 minutes, glaze with icing.

For the icing: Combine all ingredients together, adding only as much milk as you need to get the desired consistency for a soft, spreadable icing. (Some people like thin icing, some like it thick.) Spread over the warm cinnamon rolls and serve.

GRAYSON'S SPINNING WHEEL

1937-1971

One of my biggest treats as a kid was when my dad would load us up in the car for a trip to the Spinning Wheel. We always went to the one in Wahouma; most people just called it the "Polar Bear" because it had sprayed icicles hanging from the building and life-sized polar bear statues out front. I was far more mesmerized by the huge billboard menu: floats, sundaes, and milkshakes in 300 flavors and 100 different combinations.

I remember staring out the back window of our station wagon, studying the list of flavors; tutti-frutti, peanut butter, butterscotch, peach, banana, cherry, strawberry, and lemon always got my attention. All of the fruit milkshakes were made with real fruit. Eventually, the car hop would show up at dad's driver window, and I'd call out "Butterscotch" from the back seat, the same thing I got every time. The car hop would return in what seemed like a year later and clip the tray of milkshakes on the window that was half rolled down. The six milkshakes would cost Dad about $3.

There were other Spinning Wheel locations around Birmingham including Lakeview, West End, and the main creamery at 801 20th Street South, but the "Polar Bear" on the eastern side of town was a Birmingham landmark until it closed.

—Martie

> **Tip:** Today, you can get Spinning Wheel milkshakes at Hamburger Heaven; they claim to use the exact recipes used way back then. The ingredients are hand-spun, the same way they used to be. You'll find chocolate, vanilla, strawberry, orange dream, peach, cherry, banana, and peanut butter on the menu. Get one for a trip down memory lane. . . you'll only miss the polar bears.

GONE BUT NOT FORGOTTEN FAVORITES

PEANUT BUTTER MILKSHAKE à la THE SPINNING WHEEL

Yield: 2 tall milkshakes

INGREDIENTS

1 cup very cold milk *(Use whole, 2%, or skim.)*

2 cups vanilla ice cream

1/2 cup creamy peanut butter

2 tablespoons malted milk powder *(Find it at most grocery stores.)*

Peanut butter chips or chopped peanuts for garnish

DIRECTIONS:

In a blender, combine all ingredients; cover and process for 30 seconds or until smooth. Add a bit more milk if the consistency is too stiff. Pour into chilled glasses and garnish with peanut butter chips or chopped peanuts; serve immediately.

Notes

ARDEN
PHOTOGRAPHY

Select images from Magic City Cravings
by Arden Ward Upton

Cocktails

Dram Whiskey Bar
▶▶ Bourbon Slush 52

The Marble Ring
▶▶ Wonderland Cocktail 54

Jinsei Sushi
▶▶ Blackberry Mojito 56

Dyron's Lowcountry
▶▶ Lowcountry Peach Daiquiri 58

The Collins Bar
▶▶ Prepare to be Boarded
▶▶ The Alabama Songbird 60

Saw's Juke Joint
▶▶ Alabama Bushwacker Cocktail 62

Brick & Tin
▶▶ Kentucky Apple Cocktail 64

Gallery Bar
▶▶ Cranberry Champagne Sparkler 66

John's City Diner
▶▶ Elder-Fashioned 68

The Louis
▶▶ The Land of G Cocktail
▶▶ Ruby Blue Cocktail 70

Little Savannah
▶▶ Heirloom Blush 72

Roots & Revelry
▶▶ Spirit of Resistance 74

DRAM WHISKEY BAR

2721 Cahaba Road
Mountain Brook, Alabama 35223
205-871-8212 | AvoRestaurant.com

ESTABLISHED: 2009

KNOWN FOR: One of the finest and most extensive fine whiskey collections in the Southeast, including a special bourbon bottled exclusively for Dram by Woodford Reserve. Proprietor Tom Sheffer tells us his grandmother used to serve this Bourbon Slush to guests on hot summer days back in his Kentucky hometown. The menu includes bar bites like Deviled Eggs, Black Angus burgers, and their addictive Truffle Parmesan Fries.

DON'T MISS: The Steak and Biscuits. House-made biscuits are rolled daily for this local favorite—a throwback to Birmingham's Ireland's Restaurant, closed long ago but still remembered fondly by many locals (Find the recipe on page 32). Its Old Fashioned is one of the best in town.

Dram Bourbon Slush

MOUNTAIN BROOK VILLAGE

DRAM BOURBON SLUSH

Yield: 30+ servings, depending on portion size.
It can be halved for a smaller crowd.

INGREDIENTS

4 cups Kentucky bourbon

12 cups water

4 cups black tea, *brewed strong*

2 cups granulated sugar

1 (12-ounce) container frozen orange juice concentrate, *thawed*

1 (12-ounce) container frozen lemon juice concentrate, *thawed*

Ice

Fresh mint sprigs for garnish

DIRECTIONS:

Mix bourbon, water, tea, and sugar with orange and lemon juice concentrates in a large bowl or other container until sugar dissolves. Pour into a series of plastic containers (or gallon freezer bags) and freeze until an hour before serving.

Place the frozen mixture in a large bowl and thaw, gently breaking it up every 10 minutes or so. Add ice (or limited amounts of water) as desired as the punch melts to achieve the desired consistency.

Serve in julep or punch cups and garnish with sprigs of mint.

Wonderland Cocktail

THE MARBLE RING

430 41st Street South, Suite B (upstairs)
Birmingham, Alabama 35222
205-202-2252 | TheMarbleRing.com

ESTABLISHED: 2016

KNOWN FOR: The hidden phone booth and a 1920s speakeasy atmosphere where you'd almost expect to see Montgomery's own Zelda Fitzgerald secreted away in one of the private seating areas, surrounded by admirers. Ascending the stairwell from the unmarked door, don't think you've gone to the wrong place when you find Hot Diggity Dogs at the top of the landing. They'll point you to the blue door where you'll request admission. Entrance will depend on several factors: how many are in the party and how crowded they are. The whole place, including the swanky silver bathtub in the center of the room, has capacity for only 50 guests.

DON'T MISS: Happy hour every weekday from 5-7 p.m. The uniquely named cocktails are inspired by a different story of the legendary Fitzgerald; most are hip adaptations of classic cocktails that incorporate house-made bitters and syrups. The Marble Ring is also the only place in Birmingham where you can drink Champagne in a bathtub in public. As F. Scott Fitzgerald once famously said, "Too much of anything is bad, but too much champagne is just right." Inspired by Zelda's paintings of scenes from Alice in Wonderland while she was in an insane asylum, the Wonderland creates an illusion of hallucination as it changes colors before your eyes.

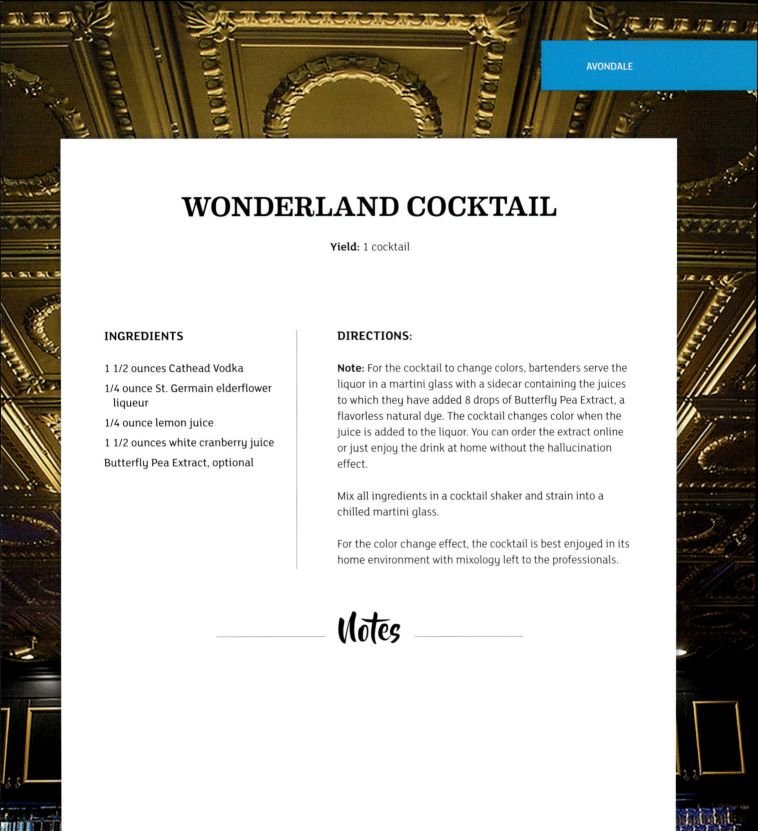

AVONDALE

WONDERLAND COCKTAIL

Yield: 1 cocktail

INGREDIENTS

1 1/2 ounces Cathead Vodka

1/4 ounce St. Germain elderflower liqueur

1/4 ounce lemon juice

1 1/2 ounces white cranberry juice

Butterfly Pea Extract, optional

DIRECTIONS:

Note: For the cocktail to change colors, bartenders serve the liquor in a martini glass with a sidecar containing the juices to which they have added 8 drops of Butterfly Pea Extract, a flavorless natural dye. The cocktail changes color when the juice is added to the liquor. You can order the extract online or just enjoy the drink at home without the hallucination effect.

Mix all ingredients in a cocktail shaker and strain into a chilled martini glass.

For the color change effect, the cocktail is best enjoyed in its home environment with mixology left to the professionals.

Notes

Blackberry Mojito

JINSEI SUSHI

1830 29th Avenue South
Homewood, Alabama 35209
205-802-1440 | JinseiSushi.com

ESTABLISHED: 2006

KNOWN FOR: The freshest sushi and sashimi and coolest cocktails in town served in a swanky, hip but casual atmosphere. Founder and former Zoës Kitchen's CEO John Cassimus wanted a local place to eat sushi to rival restaurants he found in larger cities. The fresh seafood is flown in daily, and the menu includes cold and hot sushi dishes. Cassimus recruited his team of sushi chefs and brought them to Birmingham to ensure an authentic sushi dining experience. The Champagne and wine selection is extensive—one of the best in town—and the restaurant often offers specials.

DON'T MISS: The Kadoma Tuna, their signature dish and everyone's favorite. Even if you don't think you like sushi, you will love it; sushi rice is fried crispy and layered with thin strips of spicy tuna, cool avocado, jalapeno, and fish roe. Tempura Green Beans are another don't-miss staple at Jinsei; delicately fried green beans are served with a house-made aioli dipping sauce that makes them completely addictive. If you do not eat seafood, try the River Rock Kobe; guests use a fiery hot stone to sear prime Kobe flank steak at the table.

HOMEWOOD

BLACKBERRY MOJITO

Yield: 1 cocktail

INGREDIENTS

Sour Mix:

2 cups granulated sugar

2 cups water

2 cups lime juice

Cocktail:

4 large mint leaves, plus a sprig for garnish

1 teaspoon granulated sugar

10 fresh blackberries, plus 2 for garnish

2 ounces rum

1 ounce club soda

DIRECTIONS:

For the Sour Mix: In a small saucepan whisk sugar and water together. Bring mixture to a boil and whisk until sugar is completely dissolved. Remove from heat and add lime juice. Refrigerate in an airtight container. The mix keeps up to 2 days.

For the cocktail: In a glass tumbler, muddle mint, sugar, and blackberries well until flavors combine and mint oil is released. Fill a glass to the rim with ice. Add rum, soda, and 3 ounces Sour Mix. Cover glass with metal shaker and vigorously shake. Pour cocktail in a highball glass and garnish with a skewer of blackberries and a sprig of mint.

Notes

DYRON'S LOWCOUNTRY

121 Oak Street
Mountain Brook, Alabama 35213
205-834-8257 | DyronsLowcountry.com

ESTABLISHED: 2009

KNOWN FOR: Farm-fresh ingredients. Whether at the bar or on the menu, Dyron's always seeks out the best ingredients possible from their farmers, fishermen, and providers. Ask what's fresh that day, and you can get a cocktail straight off the tree. Chilton County peaches which make an appearance on the menu in the late spring and last until late July.

DON'T MISS: The gumbo (See the recipe on page 128). Dyron's Sunday brunch paired with their famous Bloody Mary is a great way to wrap up the weekend. If you're going with the Creole Jumbo Shrimp and Grits, get started with some oysters or maybe the West Indies Salad. Add some beignets for dessert; they are served with warm chocolate sauce and strawberry cream cheese. If you're in the mood for breakfast, the Cinnamon Raisin French Toast is the way to go, and add an order of Conecuh sausage or Applewood bacon.

Lowcountry Peach Daiquiri

CRESTLINE VILLAGE

LOWCOUNTRY PEACH DAIQUIRI

Yield: 1 cocktail

INGREDIENTS

- 1 lime, cut in half and juiced
- 2 ounces fresh-squeezed Chilton County peach juice *(about 3 peaches)*
- 1 1/2 ounces Mount Gay rum
- Lime slice and mint spring for garnish

DIRECTIONS:

Fill a shaker with ice, lime juice, peach juice, and Mount Gay rum. Shake for 5-10 seconds. Strain over ice and serve. Garnish with a lime wedge and a sprig of mint.

Notes

The Alabama Songbird

Prepare to be Boarded

THE COLLINS BAR

2125 2nd Avenue North
Birmingham, Alabama 35203
205-323-7995 | TheCollinsBar.com

ESTABLISHED: 2012

KNOWN FOR: Hipsters, business execs, creative types, and lawyers who hang out at this loft district watering hole where the cocktails are as unique as the vibe. Don't ask for a cocktail menu because there is not one; the bartenders craft cocktails to order based on what you're in the mood for that day. The bar's Prepare to be Boarded, however, is an Old Fashioned variation with notes of apple, vanilla, and almond.

DON'T MISS: The grub. Known for swanky, trendy libations, the bar menu is just as edgy; think familiar comfort food with a first-class upgrade. You'll find tater tots fried in bacon fat and pigs in-a-blanket made with bourbon-glazed pork belly.

PREPARE to be BOARDED

Yield: 1 cocktail

INGREDIENTS

- 1 ounce Hamilton 86 Guyana Rum
- 1/2 ounce Ron Matusalem 10 Year Gold Dominican Republic Rum
- 1/2 ounce Laird's 100 Proof Apple Brandy
- 1/2 teaspoon Velvet Falernum *(a liqueur with notes of lime, almond, vanilla, ginger, and clove)*
- 1/2 teaspoon Orgeat *(You can substitute almond syrup if necessary.)*
- 8 drops Bittermen's Xocolate Mole Bitters
- 1 thin strip lemon peel

DIRECTIONS:

Combine all ingredients except lemon peel in a mixing glass and stir to chill, mix, and dilute. Strain into an Old Fashioned glass filled with ice or serve straight up. Zest the peel over the drink, taking care to express oils into cocktail.

THE ALABAMA SONGBIRD

Yield: 1 cocktail

INGREDIENTS

- 1 1/2 ounces Cana Brava Panamanian Rum *(Cuban style may be substituted.)*
- 1/4 ounce Yellow Chartreuse
- 3/4 ounce fresh-squeezed lemon juice
- 1/2 ounce Passion Fruit Syrup *(Real passionfruit juice can be substituted.)*
- 2 dashes Angostura bitters
- Champagne or Cava
- 1 thin strip of orange peel for garnish

DIRECTIONS:

Combine all ingredients except orange peel and Champagne in a shaking tin and shake briskly for a few seconds. Strain over ice into a Collins glass. Top with crisp dry Champagne or Cava.

Express (squeeze) orange peel over the top to release the oils and enjoy.

Taylor Hicks filming *State Plate* at Saw's

SAW'S JUKE JOINT

1115 Dunston Avenue
Birmingham, Alabama 35213
205-745-3920 | SawsBBQ.com

ESTABLISHED: 2012

KNOWN FOR: A great neighborhood vibe paired with Saw's legendary barbecue and cool music from local artists. Oh, yeah, our own American Idol and Saw's Juke Joint partner Taylor Hicks occasionally sits in on tunes when he's in town. The menu is a riff on Saw's Soul Kitchen favorites with specials exclusive to the Juke Joint. Everyone raves about the Bushwacker, and many customers have asked for the recipe. A Bushwacker is a frozen, creamy cocktail typically served in bars along Alabama's Gulf coast. Since the Juke Joint uses a commercial freezer for their Bushwackers, you'll have to stop in if you want the exact drink, but you can make this version at home.

DON'T MISS: The wings. Taylor swears they are the best in town and beyond, and with his new television show, State Plate, he should know! Pair the wings with an order of the fried pickles for the perfect tangy-sweet bite. The Stuffed Taters are a house specialty; big baked potatoes are loaded with tons of toppings. Saw's BBQ has found national recognition on Food Network and within the pages of *Garden & Gun* and *Southern Living*, too. If you haven't already, you're going to want to try Saw's Pork N'Greens. An eternal Birmingham favorite, find it on page 154.

Alabama Bushwacker Cocktail

ALABAMA BUSHWACKER COCKTAIL

Yield: 2-4 cocktails, depending on portion size

INGREDIENTS

1 pint vanilla ice cream

1/2 cup half-and-half

2 ounces light rum, *chilled*

1 ounce coconut rum, *chilled*

1 ounce Kahlua (coffee liqueur), *chilled*

1 ounce Baileys Irish Crème, *chilled*

1 ounce crème de cacao liqueur, *chilled*

Whipped cream, chocolate syrup, or maraschino cherry for garnish, *optional*

DIRECTIONS:

Note: The result is best if all the ingredients are chilled. Use a short rocks glass for a liquid dessert or after dinner drink; top with whipped cream or a drizzle of chocolate syrup if desired.

In a blender, add all the ingredients except the garnish. Blend on high for 10 seconds or until combined and slushy.

Pour into chilled glasses. Garnish as desired.

Note: If you don't have a blender, you can use an immersion blender or even a large Mason jar to make this cocktail. For the Mason jar, simply add all the ingredients and shake.

Notes

BRICK & TIN

Mountain Brook Village
2901 Cahaba Road
Mountain Brook, Alabama 35223
205-502-7971 | BrickAndTin.com

Downtown
214 20th Street North
Birmingham, Alabama 35203
205-297-8636 | BrickAndTin.com

ESTABLISHED: Downtown 2010, Mountain Brook 2014

KNOWN FOR: Quality straight-from-the-farm cuisine in a fast casual setting plus seasonal craft cocktails, a well-stocked bar, and ample wine list at the Mountain Brook location. Locally sourced ingredients make for the freshest salads and soups.

DON'T MISS: Sunday brunch, with fresh-baked pastries that change weekly. If you like sweet, try the French Toast. If you prefer savory, order the Breakfast Sandwich with egg, city ham, apple butter, and cheddar. Brunch is only served at the Mountain Brook location.

Kentucky Apple Cocktail

MOUNTAIN BROOK VILLAGE AND DOWNTOWN

KENTUCKY APPLE COCKTAIL

Yield: 1 cocktail

INGREDIENTS

Cinnamon Syrup:

1 small cinnamon stick

1 cup water

1 cup granulated sugar

1 1/2 ounces bourbon

1/2 teaspoon lemon juice plus a scant pinch of lemon zest

2 dashes bitters

Splash of apple juice *(Brick & Tin uses homemade, but you may substitute Simply Apple.)*

Twist of lemon, slice of apple, and/or grated cinnamon and clove for garnish

DIRECTIONS:

Note: Cinnamon syrup requires 24-hour advance prep.

For the Cinnamon Syrup: Toast cinnamon stick in a dry pan to release the oil and enhance the cinnamon flavor. Heat the water in a pot. Add the sugar, bring to a boil, and remove from the heat, stirring to dissolve the sugar completely. Add the toasted cinnamon stick. Leave the cinnamon stick in the syrup overnight, stored in the refrigerator.

To serve: Fill a 10-ounce rocks glass with ice. In a shaker combine the bourbon, 1/4 ounce (1 1/2 teaspoons) Cinnamon Syrup, lemon juice and zest, and bitters. Shake well. Pour over the ice and top with apple juice.

Lemon, apple, or grated cinnamon and/or clove can be added for garnish if more flavor is desired.

Notes

GALLERY BAR

1930 Cahaba Road
Mountain Brook, Alabama 35223
205-870-8404 | VinoBirmingham.com

ESTABLISHED: 2015

KNOWN FOR: A carefully curated collection of wines, cocktails, and art in a sleek, elegant gallery setting right next door to neighborhood veteran Vino, its stylish sister. Gallery Bar is the perfect spot to start or end a date. It is also a fun place to go with the girls or to get dressed up and meet for drinks at the bar to celebrate a new job, engagement, or each other.

DON'T MISS: Anything served in a Champagne coupe; it makes any drink feel sophisticated. The menu changes frequently, but you'll always find a version of a Martini, Old Fashioned, or Manhattan in addition to one of the best Whiskey Sours in town. The Cranberry Champagne Sparkler is so popular during the holidays that many guests have asked for the recipe. Add a chilled platter of freshly shucked oysters for the perfect beginning to any evening.

Cranberry Champagne Sparkler

ENGLISH VILLAGE

CRANBERRY CHAMPAGNE SPARKLER

Yield: 2 cocktails

INGREDIENTS

1/4 cup fresh cranberries
1/2 cup cranberry juice cocktail
2 lime wedges
Prosecco, Champagne, or Cava

DIRECTIONS:

Freeze whole cranberries on a sheet tray. Place about 3-4 of the frozen cranberries in the bottom of each Champagne glass. Fill the glass 3/4 full with cranberry juice cocktail and squeeze in a wedge of lime juice. Top with a dry sparkling wine: Prosecco, Champagne, or Cava.

Notes

JOHN'S CITY DINER

112 Richard Arrington Jr. Boulevard North
Birmingham, Alabama 35203
205-322-6014 | JohnsCityDiner.com

ESTABLISHED: The original John's Restaurant, owned and made a local legend by John Proferis, the late father of Zoës Kitchen founder Zoë Cassimus, opened in 1944. The current owners, Shannon and Shana Gober, bought it in 2004.

KNOWN FOR: Southern favorites with a modern twist. Menu favorites include the Not Your Mama's Macaroni & Cheese in three versions and Chicken and Waffles in original and Hong Kong style. The Fudge Farms chops are brined and grilled to order with a bourbon-maple glaze.

DON'T MISS: The extensive selection of Alabama craft beers and fine bourbon. The bar snacks have been developed to accompany the bar menu and are celebrated with daily happy hour specials. Try a coffee cocktail like the Chocolate Almond or a drinkable dessert like the Chocolate Martini. Its new take on the Old Fashioned, the Elder-Fashioned, leaves out the sugar and replaces it with elderflower liqueur.

Elder-Fashioned

DOWNTOWN

ELDER-FASHIONED

Yield: 1 cocktail

INGREDIENTS

1 fresh orange slice

1 fresh cherry

2 dashes orange bitters *(Fee Brothers is preferred.)*

1 ounce St. Germaine Elderflower liqueur

2 ounces whiskey of your choice *(John's uses Woodford Bourbon.)*

Ice

Orange slice and cherry for garnish

DIRECTIONS:

In a tall glass or cocktail shaker, muddle the orange and cherry with the bitters and St. Germaine, using a wooden spoon or muddler.

Add the bourbon and pour over ice. Garnish with an orange slice and a cherry.

(Above) The Land of G Cocktail (Right) Ruby Blue Cocktail

THE LOUIS @ THE PIZITZ FOOD HALL

1821 2nd Ave North
Birmingham, Alabama 35203
thepizitz.com/food-hall

ESTABLISHED: 2017

KNOWN FOR: Vintage ambiance meets urban glamour at The Louis, a spot reminiscent of craft cocktail bars found in New York or Chicago. The newly renovated multi-use Pizitz building features residences on the top floors and a food hall on the first floor. The hub of it all is The Louis, a bar named after Louis Pizitz, the original owner of the building that housed his family's eponymous department store back in the day. Mixologists at The Louis are highly trained and armed with a vast repertoire of classic cocktails and fashionable on-trend hipster favorites.

DON'T MISS: The people watching. The Louis is a great place to have a drink before meandering off to one of the food stalls for dinner. While you are at it, check out the bartenders as they shake, stir, blend, and pour up cocktails like Ruby Blue, made with Green Chartreuse, a timeless French liqueur made by Carthusian Monks. The Land of G cocktail is named for a song from the 1930s about Grapico soda called "The Land of Grapico." Back then, the bottler would send out the sheet music to the song upon request.

DOWNTOWN

THE LAND of G COCKTAIL

Yield: 1 cocktail

INGREDIENTS

3/4 ounce gin

3/4 ounce bourbon

3/4 once Cynar liqueur

1/2 ounce lemon juice

2 ounces Grapico soda

Lemon twist for garnish

DIRECTIONS:

Combine all ingredients except the Grapico and lemon twist in a cocktail shaker. Shake and strain over ice into a Collins glass. Top with a Grapico float and garnish with a lemon twist.

RUBY BLUE COCKTAIL

Yield: 1 cocktail

INGREDIENTS

Laphraoig (single malt Scotch whiskey), for rinse

1 1/2 ounces Silver Tequila

1/2 ounce Green Chartreuse liqueur

3/4 ounce Cocchi Americano Rosa liqueur

1 sage leaf for garnish

DIRECTIONS:

Chill a classic coup glass. Rinse the glass with Laphraoig and discard it. In a mixing glass stir together tequila, Chartreuse, and Rosa, and strain into the prepared coup. Rub the sage leaf to release its essential oils and delicately float it on top of the cocktail.

LITTLE SAVANNAH RESTAURANT AND BAR

3811 Clairmont Avenue
Birmingham, Alabama 35222
205-591-1119 | LittleSavannah.com

ESTABLISHED: 2003

KNOWN FOR: Craft cocktails like the Cherry Poppins cocktail (recipe is featured in *Birmingham's Best Bites*). The creative bar program has the same standards as the restaurant with seasonal offerings based on what the farmers daily bring in the door. The wine list is quite good, and an extensive after-dinner drink menu invites guests to linger over a cordial, Port, or French-press coffee after dinner. The Heirloom Blush is a light, refreshing Bloody Mary alternative with true tomato flavor.

DON'T MISS: Sunday brunch. It is offered monthly by invitation or reservation only. There is limited seating, so you'll have to call to get on the list. Try Chef Clifton Holt's Eggs Benedict or Corned Beef Hash.

Heirloom Blush

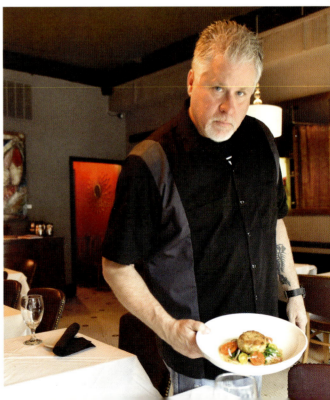

FOREST PARK

HEIRLOOM BLUSH

Yield: 2 cocktails

INGREDIENTS

2 tablespoons kosher salt

2 tablespoons Tabasco, divided

1 heirloom tomato, *sliced 1/2-inch thick*

2 slices cucumber

5 leaves fresh basil

2 leaves fresh cilantro

3 ounces Cathead vodka

3 dashes celery bitters *(Fee Brothers Bitters was used for this recipe.)*

Dash lemon and lime juice

Ice

Tomato and lime for garnish

DIRECTIONS:

For the Tabasco salt: On a plate, mix kosher salt with 1 tablespoon Tabasco. Spread out and allow to dry for a few hours. (Put into a warm oven to expedite if necessary.) Set aside until ready to serve.

In a cocktail shaker, muddle a pinch of the Tabasco salt, 2-3 tomato slices, cucumber, basil, and cilantro with a muddler or wooden spoon. Be sure to bruise the basil leaves. Add the vodka, bitters, lemon and lime juices, and ice. Shake until well chilled. Taste, check seasoning, and add more salt or Tabasco as desired.

To serve: Run a lemon around the rim of two rocks glasses; dip the rim into the Tabasco salt. Fill glasses with ice and strain the cocktail into the glasses. Garnish with a halved tomato slice and lime wheel.

Notes

ROOTS & REVELRY

1623 2nd Avenue North, Suite B
Birmingham, Alabama 35203
205-730-1907 | Roots-Revelry.com

ESTABLISHED: 2017

KNOWN FOR: A fun spin on American cuisine in an incredible setting with amazing skyline views. Owner and Executive Chef Brandon Cain has been waiting a long time to create his signature restaurant in Birmingham, and it has been worth the wait. Opened in early 2017 in the newly renovated Thomas Jefferson Tower, the setting is sleek and swanky but completely comfortable. The menu is too. Chef Cain is known for the ultimate in comfort food from his ventures at Saw's Soul Kitchen and Post Office Pies. Here, he elegantly transforms comfort food favorites into posh dishes like Roots' PB&J: a crisp pork belly with cashew butter and quince jelly.

DON'T MISS: The aforementioned PB&J, Grilled Octopus, and the NY Strip already have a legion of fans and repeat customers. Save room for dessert; the Milk and Cookies is a riff on the Dominique Ansel version and just as good. An oatmeal raisin cookie is shaped into a shot glass, filled with milk, and served with Bananas Foster sauce and Brulee' banana. If you get a chance, stop in for Sunday brunch. The bartenders make a mean Bloody Mary, and the biscuits and gravy are second to none.

Roots & Revelry's Spirit of Resistance

DOWNTOWN

ROOTS & REVELRY'S SPIRIT of RESISTANCE

Yield: 1 cocktail

INGREDIENTS

1 1/2 ounces tequila

3/4 ounce lime juice

1 ounce pineapple juice

1/2 ounce Campari

1 drop Bitterman's Hellfire Shrub

Jalapeño salt (or other seasoned pepper salt) for garnish

DIRECTIONS:

Use a lime or water to moisten the rim of the glass. Dip 1/4 of rim in the jalapeño salt. Add ingredients to a cocktail shaker filled with ice. Shake until well chilled and pour into the prepared glass.

Notes

Appetizers & Breads

Bamboo on 2nd
▸▸ Momos 78

Chez Fonfon
▸▸ Tartine Provençale 80

The Great Wall
▸▸ Dan Dan Noodle 82

Bottega
▸▸ Arancini with Sicilian Tomato Sauce 84

Slice Pizza & Brewhouse
▸▸ Fire-Baked Chicken Wings 86

The Pita Stop
▸▸ Hummus 88

Sky Castle Gastro Lounge
▸▸ Pork Belly and Fried Oysters 90

Rib-It-Up
▸▸ Cracklin' Muffins 92

Century Restaurant & Bar
▸▸ Pimento Cheese Fritters 94

Nabeel's Café & Market
▸▸ Feta Theologos 96

Avo Restaurant
▸▸ Avo Dip 98

Momos (Nepali Meat Dumplings)

BAMBOO ON 2ND

2212 2nd Avenue North
Birmingham, Alabama 35203
205-703-0551 | BambooOn2nd.com

ESTABLISHED: 2015

KNOWN FOR: Momos, the Nepali meat dumplings of former Chef Abhi Sainju's youth. His ramen bowls seasoned with pork broth have a cult following, too. Diners love the small plates-perfect for sharing. The fried green beans with Togarashi sauce are a favorite as is the Grilled Edamame with Himalayan Sherpa pink salt. Bamboo is also known for unique dishes like Smoked Unagi-a Japanese freshwater eel and one of the most diverse sushi menus in town.

DON'T MISS: The sushi rolls! Also Bamboo's spin on fried chicken, the Kathmandu Fried Chicken Lollipop served with the house sweet sauce. At the bar, try the Gin-Gin: Bombay Dry Gin, Canton ginger liqueur, soda, and lemon or a bottle of their select sake.

DOWNTOWN

BAMBOO on 2ND MOMOS
(Nepali Meat Dumplings)

Yield: Serves 3-4

INGREDIENTS

Momos:

1 pound ground turkey

1 cup red onions, *diced*

2 teaspoons ground coriander

1 teaspoon ground cumin

2 tablespoons cilantro, *chopped*

2 tablespoons scallions, *chopped*

2 tablespoons soy sauce

2 tablespoons olive oil

1 teaspoon salt

2 teaspoons garlic paste

2 teaspoons ginger paste
  (Find it in the Asian aisle.)

1 package dumpling wrappers
  (Store-bought is fine; they are
  usually in the refrigerated section.)

1/2 cup hot water

Momo Sauce:

1 tablespoon olive oil

2 cups diced tomatoes

5-6 garlic cloves

1 Thai chili

2 teaspoons sesame seeds

Salt to taste

Juice from 1/2 a lime

1 tablespoon cilantro, *chopped*

DIRECTIONS:

Mix Momos ingredients (excluding the wrappers and hot water) in a large bowl and let marinate for half an hour.

For the sauce: In a saucepan, heat the olive oil. Add all the ingredients except the lime juice and the cilantro; sauté for about 5 minutes. Transfer to a blender (or use an immersion blender) to blend well. Squeeze in the lime juice. Sprinkle with cilantro. Set aside for service.

To assemble: Take one dumpling skin at a time and brush water around the edges. Place a spoonful of the turkey mixture in middle. Fold in half. Pinch the edges of each side together, leaving no air pockets inside. Steam all the dumplings in a bamboo or basket steamer for 15-20 minutes.

Note: If a steamer is not available, carefully drop the Momos into a pot of boiling water like you would ravioli. When they float to the top of the water, they are done. Drain and serve with Momo Sauce. After the Momos are steamed, you may also pan fry until golden brown.

To serve: Pour the sauce over the Momos or serve on the side as a dip.

CHEZ FONFON

Chef Frank Stitt, James Beard Award Winner

2007 11th Avenue South
Birmingham, Alabama 35205
205-939-3221 | FonfonBham.com

ESTABLISHED: 2000

KNOWN FOR: Rustic French fare. You feel like you're in Paris from the moment you enter the door. This charming bistro in the heart of Southside features a great bar with some of the best bartenders in town crafting old school cocktails like the French Blonde, a local favorite. The Hamburger Fonfon is consistently ranked the No. 1 burger in Birmingham.

DON'T MISS: The Charcuterie, beautifully presented with housemade pâté, rillettes, and cured meats. The catch of the day is always perfectly cooked. Save room for dessert; don't miss the Coconut Cake, any of the seasonal tarts, or the dense, rich Pots de Crème or the lemon meringue tart, one of my personal cravings. I hang out at Chez Fonfon so often that I call it my office.
- Martie

Tartine Provençale

SOUTHSIDE

CHEZ FONFON TARTINE PROVENÇALE
Toasted Sourdough with Goat Cheese and Tapenade

Yield: Serves 8 as a hors d'oeuvre or snack

INGREDIENTS

2 cloves garlic, *divided*

2 anchovy fillets

1/4 cup capers

1 cup black olives *(Kalamata or Green Cerigonla)*

1 teaspoon brandy or rum of your choice

8 slices fresh sourdough bread

1/2 cup extra-virgin olive oil

Kosher salt and black pepper to taste

1/4 pound fresh, local goat cheese

Fresh basil or marjoram for garnish

DIRECTIONS:

Heat grill or grill pan to about 350° Fahrenheit.

In a mortar, use a pestle to crush 1 clove of garlic and the anchovy fillets together until they have the consistency of a paste. Add the capers and olives and pound in the mortar or transfer to food processor to make a coarse purèe. Add the brandy and drizzle in olive oil. Crush the other clove of garlic and set aside.

Brush fresh sourdough slices with olive oil on both sides and then place on a hot grill. Grill the slices on either side until thoroughly toasted, and then rub both sides with a clove of crushed garlic. Season with salt and pepper.

Spread the goat cheese onto the warm sourdough bread and garnish each slice with a dollop of tapenade. Place the tartines onto a small plate with the three points touching in the center and garnish with basil or marjoram.

THE GREAT WALL

706 Valley Avenue
Birmingham, Alabama 35209
205-945-1465 | GreatWallBirmingham.com

ESTABLISHED: 1982

KNOWN FOR: Authentic cuisine of Shanghai, China, known as Sichuan-style Chinese cuisine. The Great Wall is one of the oldest Chinese restaurants in Birmingham. You'll find authentic hot pot and Hibachi dishes on the menu along with American-Chinese standards like Mongolian Beef and Egg Foo Young. Some regular customers have been dining at The Great Wall for over 30 years and have seen the restaurant through three owners and a devastating fire. The current owner, Sunny, has been a fixture since 1994. Be sure to say hello to her.

DON'T MISS: Soup dumplings or Bao, little pork pouches filled with heavenly broth like you find in New York. Bite the dumpling, suck out the broth, and then eat the dumpling. They come steamed or pan fried. You'll become addicted, so go ahead and put the take-out number in your phone.

Dan Dan Noodle

DAN DAN NOODLE
Vegetarian and Pork Version

Yield: 1 serving as an appetizer

INGREDIENTS

6 ounce soft noodles *(Find these in the Asian aisle or at an Asian market.)*

1/2 teaspoon granulated sugar

1 teaspoon soy sauce

1 clove garlic, *crushed*

1 teaspoon of sesame paste

Drizzle of each: chili pepper oil, rice vinegar, and sesame oil

1 green onion, *thinly sliced*

Ground pork *(optional)*

Chinese pickled mustard *(optional)*

DIRECTIONS:

Boil soft noodles until fully cooked. Drain the water. Chill noodles with tap water, drain again, and then set noodles in a bowl.

In a separate bowl, mix all remaining ingredients except green onion together and pour the mixture into the noodle bowl. Mix together and garnish with green onions on top.

For a richer body and zesty flavor, add ground pork and Chinese pickled mustard. Brown the meat in a bit of oil and drain. Mix with the mustard and combine with the noodles.

Arancini with Sicilian Tomato Sauce

BOTTEGA

2240 Highland Avenue South
Birmingham, Alabama 35205
205-939-1000 | BottegaRestaurant.com/Bottega

ESTABLISHED: 1988

KNOWN FOR: Italian cuisine, Stitt style. Bottega's stately limestone façade faces a garden patio set with tables for dining alfresco. The main dining room at Bottega is romantic and elegant, a wonderful place to impress a date or celebrate a special occasion. Chef Frank Stitt's menu is influenced by Italy and recreated here with the freshest local ingredients available. For the Arancini, Bottega adds the flavors of the Eastern Mediterranean, cumin, fennel seed, and saffron to a basic tomato sauce that can be used for pasta, pizza, or dipping sauce.

DON'T MISS: The handcrafted pastas, which vary daily. Beef Carpaccio with Horseradish Cream and shaved Parmigiano have been on the menu forever and for good reason. The light and delicate Frito Misto appetizer serves up fried Gulf shrimp, oysters, and snapper with enough to share. Save room for homemade desserts created by James Beard Award Best Pastry Chef semifinalist Dolester Miles. Order a pint of Bottega ice cream to take home!

SOUTHSIDE

ARANCINI with SICILIAN TOMATO SAUCE

Yield: Approximately 20 as hors d'oeuvres or snack

INGREDIENTS

Arancini:

2 cups cooked risotto *(Follow package instructions; you may make this a day ahead.)*

1/2 cup fresh mozzarella, *cut into 1/2-inch cubes*

1/2 cup all-purpose flour

2 eggs, *broken into a bowl and whisked vigorously with 1 tablespoon water*

1 cup breadcrumbs made from cubed and ground stale bread, *crusts removed*

2 cups vegetable oil for frying *(such as sunflower oil)*

1 package dumpling wrappers

Sicilian Tomato Sauce:

2 tablespoons olive oil

2 large sweet onions, *finely chopped*

1 small carrot, *peeled and finely chopped*

1 celery stalk, *finely chopped*

2 garlic cloves, *crushed*

1/4 teaspoon cumin seed, *toasted and ground*

1/4 teaspoon fennel seed

1 dried chili pepper

1 sprig thyme

1 bay leaf

Small pinch saffron threads

3 pounds tomatoes, *quartered and seeded (or 1 (28-ounce) can peeled Roma tomatoes)*

Salt, pepper, and a pinch of sugar, if desired, to taste

Basil, parsley, or chives for garnish

DIRECTIONS:

For the Arancini: Form the risotto into ping-pong ball-sized rounds. With your finger, make an opening to the center, and place one cube of mozzarella inside. Press the rice to close. Roll the ball in flour and shake off excess. Roll in the egg wash; then roll in the breadcrumbs. Place on a rack until ready to fry. (Note: You may make these up to 6 hours ahead.)

For the Sicilian Tomato Sauce: In a large saucepan, heat olive oil until warm. Add onions and soften 5 minutes. Add carrot and celery and cook, stirring with a wooden spoon for about 5 minutes. Add garlic, cumin, fennel, chili, thyme, bay leaf, and saffron; cook for 2 minutes. Add tomatoes and season to taste. Simmer partially covered over low to medium heat for 30 minutes. Transfer to a food mill or use a food processor or immersion blender to puree. Adjust seasonings. Set aside.

To fry the Arancini: In a large skillet, heat 2 cups vegetable oil to 350° Fahrenheit. Use an appropriate thermometer to check the oil temperature. Fry the prepared Arancini in the hot oil until golden brown, about 3 to 4 minutes. Do not overcrowd the skillet. Drain on paper towels.

To serve: Cut in half, if desired, and serve atop Sicilian Tomato Sauce with herb garnish.

Fire-Baked Chicken Wings

SLICE PIZZA & BREWHOUSE

725 29th Street South
Birmingham, Alabama 35233
205-715-9300 | SliceBirmingham.com

ESTABLISHED: 2011

KNOWN FOR: Handcrafted pizza with ingredients proudly sourced from local farms. Started by brothers Jeff, Chris, and Jason Bajalieh, the family behind Sol's Deli and Sky Castle, Slice has become a fixture in Lakeview. Slice even has its own music festival, SliceFest. The White Shadow pizza (garlic, caramelized onion, portobella, and truffle oil) and the Lakeview, topped with braised short ribs, are two of their most popular pies. While the pizza takes center stage, fire-baked wings at Slice are considered the city's best by many fans.

DON'T MISS: The Little Piggy pizza, fully loaded with every kind of pork imaginable, including capicola ham, Italian sausage, prosciutto, and bacon. There's a vast selection of local craft brews and a full bar with craft cocktails. Try the artisanal cheese board, perfect to share. The S'more Calzones are warm and gooey goodness; leave plenty of room for a bite.

LAKEVIEW

SLICE PIZZA & BREWHOUSE'S FIRE-BAKED CHICKEN WINGS

Yield: 8 servings

INGREDIENTS

1 quart fresh squeezed lime juice

3/4 cup salt, *divided*

4 pounds jumbo chicken wings

1 cup extra-virgin olive oil

1/4 cup cayenne pepper

DIRECTIONS:

Open a large zip-top bag and add the lime juice, 1/2 cup salt, and chicken. Shake to coat. Place in a dish or bowl and place in the refrigerator. Soak wings 12 hours, turning the wings occasionally.

When you are ready to cook, remove and coat wings with olive oil. Toss well with 1/4 cup salt and cayenne.

Preheat grill and preheat oven to 350° Fahrenheit. Grill wings without burning. While still hot, toss wings in your favorite hot sauce, cover, and bake at 350° for 15 minutes.

Serve with your favorite ranch or blue cheese dressing.

Notes

THE PITA STOP

Southside
1106 12th Street South
Birmingham, Alabama 35205
205-328-2749 | ThePitaStop.com

Cahaba Heights
3908 Crosshaven Drive
Vestavia Hills, Alabama 35243
205-969-7482 | ThePitaStop.com

ESTABLISHED: 1981

KNOWN FOR: Kabobs: lamb, steak, chicken, seafood, vegetable, or kafta. The chicken kabob features perfectly grilled and juicy chicken, alternating with onion, tomato, and peppers. The Pita Stop hummus was one of the first of its kind in Birmingham, and even though you can now readily find hummus at other restaurants and grocery stores, it remains a local favorite to this day.

DON'T MISS: The chicken kabob. Order it with the tabbouleh instead of the salad. The combination appetizer serves up hummus (chickpea) and babaghanouj (eggplant) dips, falafel, olives, tomato slices, cucumbers, feta cheese, and pita bread. The Rolled Grape Leaves are as good as you'll find outside of the Mediterranean. This has been my family's favorite place to eat since it opened.
- Martie

Pita Stop Hummus

SOUTHSIDE AND CAHABA HEIGHTS

PITA STOP HUMMUS

Yield: Serves 8

INGREDIENTS

2 (15-ounce) cans chickpeas

2 cloves garlic

1/4 cup lemon juice

1/4 cup tahini *(sesame paste; find it on the international or Asian aisle)*

Salt to taste

Paprika for garnish

Olive oil for garnish

DIRECTIONS:

Drain juice from one can of chickpeas; leave the juice in the other can. Combine all ingredients, except for salt, in a blender or food processor.

Puree for three minutes or until smooth. Check the seasoning, and add salt to taste.

Garnish with paprika and olive oil. Serve with sliced pita bread.

Notes

Sky Castle Pork Belly and Fried Oysters with Sriracha Aioli

SKY CASTLE GASTRO LOUNGE

2808 7th Avenue South
Birmingham, Alabama 35233
205-578-6080 | SkyCastleBham.com

ESTABLISHED: 2015

KNOWN FOR: Sports served with comfort food and old-school favorites like meatloaf and fried chicken with buttermilk mashed potatoes. In the 1950s, the location was home to the locally renowned Ed Salem's Drive In. A glass DJ booth, called the sky castle, towered above the parking lot where customers placed orders with carhops on roller skates as they waited for the DJs to spin their requests. (The recipe for Ed Salem's Ice Box Pie is found on page 40.)

DON'T MISS: The Sky Castle burger with bacon jam and caramelized onions or the brunch on Saturday featuring sweet tea-brined Chicken and Waffles or the homemade biscuits and Conecuh sausage gravy.

SKY CASTLE PORK BELLY and FRIED OYSTERS with SRIRACHA AIOLI

Yield: Serves 6

INGREDIENTS

5 pounds pork belly

Salt and pepper to taste

1 1/2 tablespoons vegetable oil (for searing)

1 cup Mirin *(Japanese rice wine, found at most grocery stores in the Asian aisle)*

2 cups soy sauce

1/4 cup sesame oil

1 gallon chicken stock or broth *(Use low-sodium if using canned broth.)*

3 white onions, *diced*

5 carrots, *diced*

5 stalks celery, *diced*

1/4 cup garlic, *minced*

2 dozen shucked oysters

3 cups whole buttermilk

4 cups yellow cornmeal

Canola oil *(for frying)*

1 1/2 cups arugula for garnish

Juice from 1/2 lemon

Sriracha Aioli:

1 cup Sriracha

4 cups mayonnaise

DIRECTIONS:

Preheat oven to 350° Fahrenheit.

Season pork belly with salt and pepper. Heat the vegetable oil in a cast iron skillet. Sear the pork belly on both sides. Remove it to a deep pan that will allow at least 3 inches of room above the pork belly.

Whisk together the Mirin, soy sauce, sesame oil, and chicken stock. Add the onion, carrot, celery, and garlic. Add this mixture to the pan with the pork belly. Wrap tightly with foil and bake at 350° for 2 1/2 hours.

Transfer the pork belly to a sheet tray and allow it to cool. Reserve the braising liquid. Press the pork belly between two sheet trays in the refrigerator for at least 4 hours. When ready to serve, strain the braising liquid into a large saucepan. Portion the pork belly into six 2 1/2-ounce slices. Add the pork belly to the braising liquid and heat over low heat.

Soak the oysters in the buttermilk for at least 15 minutes. While the oysters are soaking, heat the canola oil in a Dutch oven or fryer to 350°. (It is best to use a thermometer to make sure the oil is at 350° before adding the oysters.) Drain and immediately dredge oysters in the cornmeal. Fry the oysters for 1 minute. Depending on the size of your fryer, you may want to work in batches. Be sure not to overcrowd the fryer as it will drop the oil temperature.

For the Sriracha Aioli: Whisk the Sriracha and the mayonnaise together. Add salt and pepper if desired.

To serve: Toss the arugula with lemon juice. Plate each slice of pork belly with 4 of the fried oysters drizzled with the Sriracha mayonnaise. Add the dressed arugula on top or to the side as desired.

RIB-IT-UP

830 1st Avenue North
Birmingham, Alabama 35203
205-328-7427 | RibItUp.com

ESTABLISHED: 1992

KNOWN FOR: Fantastic barbecue and soul food sides. Brothers Lewell, Lee, and Rufus Taylor started Rib-It-Up as a family business. Today, it is a father-daughter operation with Lewell and his daughter Brittney getting a lot of praise for their 'que; they have been featured as one of the top barbecue spots in the country by *USA Today*. Huge barbecue-stuffed bakers, fried fish specials, and the pork cracklin' stuffed muffins are favorites, but it is their ribs that have folks lined up.

DON'T MISS: Rib tips! Rib-It-Up is one of the few places in Birmingham to serve this specialty, which many experts say is the best bite of barbecue there is. Yams are another unique item; not too many places serve them and few do it as well as Rib-It-Up. Save room for dessert, too.

Cracklin' Muffins

CRACKLIN' MUFFINS

Yield: 12-15 muffins

INGREDIENTS

4 ounces unsalted butter

2 cups whole buttermilk

1 cup water

2 eggs

1/2 cup mayonnaise

3 cups self-rising white cornmeal

1 1/2 cups self-rising flour

1/4 cup granulated sugar

1/4 pound pork cracklin' *(Find cracklin' in the meat department or ask the butcher.)*

Non-stick spray

DIRECTIONS:

Preheat oven to 375° Fahrenheit.

Melt the butter. Add the buttermilk, water, eggs, mayonnaise, cornmeal, flour, and sugar to mixing bowl. Add the melted butter and whisk briskly. Fold in the pork cracklin'.

Spray muffin pan with non-stick spray and pour batter into pan, filling each cup about 2/3 full. Bake at 375° for 25 minutes.

Note: To make regular cornbread, follow same directions but omit the pork cracklin'.

Pimento Cheese Fritters with Pepper Jelly

CENTURY RESTAURANT & BAR

Tutwiler Hotel
2021 Park Place
Birmingham, Alabama 35203
205-458-9707 | CenturyBirmingham.com

ESTABLISHED: 2009

KNOWN FOR: Its location in a Birmingham landmark and a great burger. Staffed with students and graduates from the culinary school at Virginia College, the restaurant and its menu reflect a dedication to culinary excellence paired with Southern tradition and recipes. (The hotel originally opened in 1914 at 20th Street and Fifth Avenue North and was demolished in 1974 to make way for a bank building. The hotel reopened in 1986 at its present location, which was also built in 1914.)

DON'T MISS: Hotel guests and regulars coming in for the Century Burger, made with a custom grind of Angus brisket and chuck topped with honey garlic aioli, grilled red onions, and cheddar cheese. Another favorite is the Gulf crab cakes made with fresh lump Gulf crab, green tomato, chow-chow, and homemade remoulade.

DOWNTOWN

PIMENTO CHEESE FRITTERS with PEPPER JELLY

Yield: 18-24 fritters, depending on the size

INGREDIENTS

Pepper Jelly:

1/2 cup light Karo syrup

1/2 cup white vinegar

1 red pepper, *diced*

1 Poblano pepper, *diced*

1/4 teaspoon red pepper flakes

Pinch of salt

Pimento Cheese Fritters:

1 pound cream cheese, *at room temperature*

1 pound cheddar cheese

1 red bell pepper, *finely diced*

1/8 cup Tabasco

Salt and pepper to taste

1 1/2 cups all-purpose flour

1 1/2 cups buttermilk *(whole or non-fat)*

1 1/2 cups Panko breadcrumbs *(Find in the Asian aisle or where they sell breadcrumbs.)*

Oil for frying *(Use canola or your favorite.)*

DIRECTIONS:

For the Pepper Jelly: Place syrup and vinegar in a saucepan over medium to medium-high heat and reduce by half until sticky. Add peppers and pepper flakes and cook until soft, about 4 minutes. Add salt and taste for seasoning. Let cool. Set aside and keep at room temperature for use. The jelly will keep in the refrigerator for up to 2 weeks.

For the fritters: Combine cheeses, bell pepper, Tabasco, and salt and pepper in a mixer fitted with the paddle attachment and blend until smooth. Use a small ice cream scoop or your hands and portion pimento cheese into the size of a golf ball. Place on a parchment paper-lined baking sheet and chill in the refrigerator for at least 30 minutes prior to frying.

To fry: Set up a breading station with the flour, buttermilk, and Panko, each in a separate shallow vessel. Dip each fritter into the flour, shaking off excess, and then dip into the buttermilk and roll in the Panko. Set aside.

Prepare a fryer or Dutch oven with oil heated to 350° Fahrenheit. Use a thermometer to monitor the temperature. Drop the fritters into the hot oil carefully, a few at a time, and fry for 2 or 3 minutes or until golden brown. Remove and place on a paper towel. Lightly season with salt while still hot.

Serve with Pepper Jelly on the side.

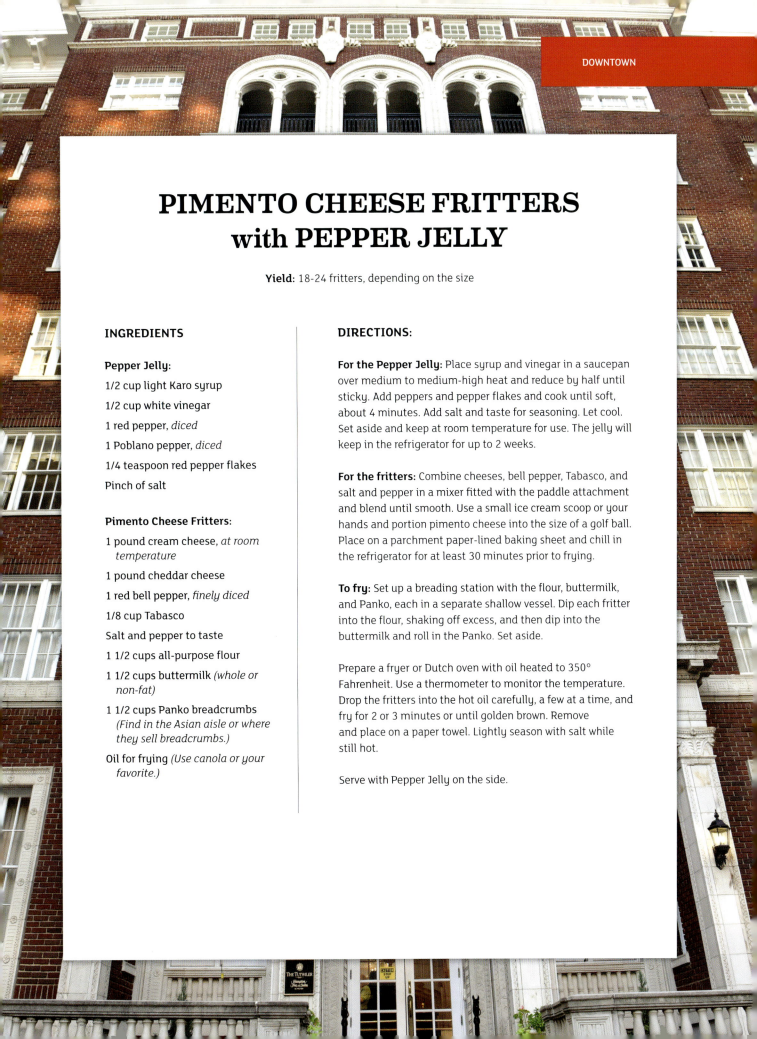

Nabeel's Feta Theologos™

NABEEL'S CAFÉ & MARKET

1706 Oxmoor Road
Homewood, Alabama 35209
205-879-9292 | Nabeels.com

ESTABLISHED: 1972

KNOWN FOR: Homemade everything. Dishes at Nabeel's are made fresh from scratch, just as they would have been in old-world Greece or Italy. What started as a market with a wide variety of imported spices, cheeses, and pastries, alongside a small café, has turned into a local institution. Families have gathered at Nabeel's for generations, and many couples had their first date there. The roast lamb has fans lining up during the holidays, and owner John Krontiras and his family will greet you personally.

DON'T MISS: Nabeel's is one of the best places in town for lamb chops and Eggplant Parmesan. Their Moussaka appears on the Alabama Tourism Department's list of 100 Dishes to Eat in Alabama Before You Die. Many requested the recipe for Nabeel's famous Feta Theologos, their most popular appetizer. At the restaurant, it comes to the table presented in foil that is whimsically shaped like a swan.

HOMEWOOD

NABEEL'S FETA THEOLOGOS™

Yield: Serves 4-5 as an appetizer

INGREDIENTS

1 (3.5-4) ounce block Feta cheese*

1/2 tablespoon extra-virgin olive oil, *plus more for drizzling*

10 garlic cloves, *finely minced*

3/4 teaspoon Greek oregano*

Italian or French sliced bread, *cut diagonally and toasted*

DIRECTIONS:

Preheat oven to 350° Fahrenheit. Cut a sheet of aluminum foil large enough to wrap the cheese, and place it on a baking sheet.

Slice cheese into a rectangle 4 inches long by 3 inches wide by 1 inch deep. Place 1/2 tablespoon olive oil in the center of the foil and feta on top of the oil. Spread the minced garlic evenly over the feta. Drizzle more olive oil on top to cover completely and sprinkle the oregano over the top.

Fold the foil around the cheese to seal it and bake at 350° for 10-12 minutes or until the cheese is bubbling. Remove from the oven and place the package on a serving plate. Carefully open the foil and add additional olive oil if needed. Serve with sliced toasted Italian or French bread.

*Use French Feta Valbresso or Greek Feta Dodonis for the best taste. Other brands of feta can be used, but the taste will be different. Valbresso Feta, Dodonis Feta, and Greek oregano are available at Nabeel's Market, next door to the restaurant. You may also substitute any type of dried oregano.

Avo Dip

AVO RESTAURANT

2721 Cahaba Road
Mountain Brook, Alabama 35223
205-871-8212 | AvoRestaurant.com

ESTABLISHED: 2009

KNOWN FOR: Avo Taco Tuesdays, complete with their signature Avo Dip and margaritas. Avo is an eclectic mix of California cuisine, southern food, and burger joint rolled into one cool spot. There's something for everyone on the menu, and you can find both fantastic happy hour bar specials and half-price bottles of wine on Sunday. The perfect location for a bridesmaid luncheon or birthday celebration; the balcony overlooks Mountain Brook Village.

DON'T MISS: The California-inspired San Diego fish tacos with lime cilantro slaw and Poblano salsa or the Steak Frites with Matchstick Fries and fried farm egg. Also the Flatbread Salad with housemade flatbread; marinated mozzarella and crushed almonds make it unique.

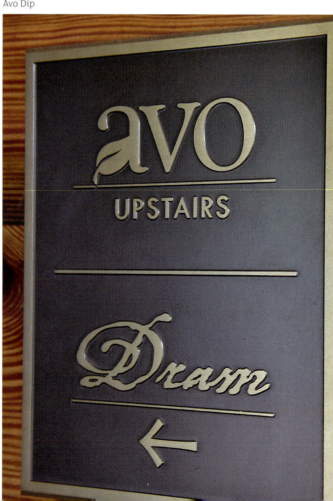

MOUNTAIN BROOK VILLAGE

AVO DIP
Guacamole Avo

Yield: About 2 cups

INGREDIENTS

2 avocados, *pitted, skinned, and mashed with a fork*

1 cup Roma tomatoes, *diced small and drained of excess water*

1 cup Poblano peppers, *diced small (about 1 pepper)*

1/4 cup yellow onion, *diced small*

1/2 tablespoon garlic, *minced fine*

2 tablespoons cilantro, *chopped*

2 tablespoons extra-virgin olive oil

1 tablespoon fresh-squeezed lime juice

1/2 tablespoon kosher salt

2 teaspoons ground black pepper

1 teaspoon granulated sugar

DIRECTIONS:

Gently mix all ingredients in a large bowl, taking care to leave some texture in the avocados. Serve with warm tortilla chips.

Note: Avo's uses house-cut and fried tortilla chips, but purchased ones will suffice.

Salads & Sides

Highlands Bar and Grill
▸▸ Tomato Salad With Cucumbers, Basil, and Lady Pea Vinaigrette 102

Bottega Café
▸▸ Bottega Bowl 104

Post Office Pies
▸▸ Brussels Sprout & Kale Salad 108

John's City Diner
▸▸ Not Your Mama's Macaroni and Cheese 110

Hot and Hot Fish Club
▸▸ Tomato Salad 112

Ovenbird
▸▸ Humitas with Charred Herb Salsa 116

Irondale Café
▸▸ Famous Fried Green Tomatoes 118

Homewood Gourmet
▸▸ Baby Blue Salad 120

Ashley Mac's
▸▸ Spinach Salad 122

Zoës Kitchen
▸▸ Live Med Salad 124

Tomato Salad with Cucumbers, Basil, and Lady Pea Vinaigrette

HIGHLANDS BAR AND GRILL

Chef Frank Stitt, James Beard Award Winner

2011 11th Avenue South
Birmingham, Alabama 35205
205-939-1400 | HighlandsBarAndGrill.com

ESTABLISHED: 1982

KNOWN FOR: Its incredible pedigree. A record nine James Beard Foundation nominations for national restaurant of the year, a win in 2001 for Chef Frank Stitt for Best Chef Southeast, and Stitt's induction into the foundation's Who's Who of Food and Beverage in America makes Highlands Bar and Grill one of the most celebrated restaurants in America. As one of the fathers of the country's farm-to-table movement, Chef Stitt's menu is constantly changing and is filled with seasonal vegetables and herbs, many from his own Paradise Farm.

DON'T MISS: The experience. Highlands is cozy, elegant, and timeless. It's a restaurant you need to revisit often since the menu changes daily. Start with the Stone Ground Baked Grits, one dish that has been on the menu since day one.

SOUTHSIDE

TOMATO SALAD with CUCUMBERS, BASIL, and LADY PEA VINAIGRETTE

Yield: Serves 4

INGREDIENTS

Vinaigrette:

1/2 cup sherry vinegar

2 shallots, *minced*

1 teaspoon thyme, *chopped*

2 teaspoons Dijon mustard

1/2 cup extra-virgin olive oil

1/2 cup canola oil

Kosher salt and freshly ground black pepper to taste

Salad:

1 pound fresh lady peas, *shelled*

1 onion, *peeled and cut in half*

1 carrot, *peeled and cut in half*

2 celery stalks, *cut in half*

3 bay leaves

3 thyme sprigs

1 teaspoon salt

1 red onion, *cut into 1/2-inch slices*

Kosher salt and freshly ground black pepper to taste

Extra-virgin olive oil

2 small cucumbers, *peeled with seeds removed, cut lengthwise into 4 strips and then into 1/4-inch dice*

2 pounds heirloom tomatoes, *preferably a variety of colors, locally sourced, cored, and thickly sliced*

2 sprigs basil, *leaves picked*

1 pint cherry tomatoes, *preferably an assortment, locally sourced, halved*

Sherry vinegar

DIRECTIONS:

For the vinaigrette: Combine sherry vinegar, shallots, and thyme in a mixing bowl, and let sit for 1 hour. Add mustard and mix well. Slowly whisk in oil and season with salt and pepper. Set aside.

For the salad: Combine the peas, onion, carrots, celery, bay leaves, thyme sprigs, and salt in a large pot; add water to cover by 3 inches, and bring to a simmer over high heat. Reduce heat to medium and allow to simmer for 20-25 minutes or until tender. Skim the foam from the peas. Set aside and allow peas to cool in liquid.

Prepare a hot grill. Season red onion with salt and pepper and drizzle with olive oil. Place onion on hot grill and slightly char, about 5 minutes on each side. Remove from grill and set aside to cool.

Drain the lady peas and add to a large mixing bowl. Cut the grilled red onion into 1/2-inch dice and add to bowl, along with cucumbers. Mix the vinaigrette well and add 1/2 cup to the lady pea mixture. Season with salt and pepper and allow 10 minutes to macerate. Place tomatoes on a sheet pan and season with salt, pepper, and the remaining vinaigrette.

On a large plate, stack the sliced heirloom tomatoes attractively, beginning with the larger slices on the bottom and alternating the lady pea vinaigrette and torn basil. Scatter cherry tomatoes over and around them, and finish with a drizzle of sherry vinegar and freshly ground black pepper.

Bottega Bowl

BOTTEGA CAFÉ

Chef Frank Stitt, James Beard Award Winner

2240 Highland Avenue South
Birmingham, Alabama 35205
205-939-1000 | BottegaRestaurant.com/Cafe

ESTABLISHED: 1988

KNOWN FOR: Casual Italian fare and a friendly vibe. The casual twin sister to posh Bottega directly next door, Bottega Café is a popular Southside lunch, drinks, and dining landmark, just as fashionable now as it was when the doors first opened. The open concept kitchen features an Old World Renato wood-fire oven, where the chefs create pizzas, steaks, fish, and other café specialties, including their craveable Café Mac & Cheese.

DON'T MISS: Chicken Scaloppini and the White Pie with fennel sausage, prosciutto, mozzarella, and crushed tomatoes, sold by the hundreds each day. The homemade desserts are also not to be missed. The Coconut Pecan Cake served with a vanilla crème anglaise has become so popular that its fans order whole cakes for holiday celebrations.

SOUTHSIDE

BOTTEGA BOWL

Yield: Serves 4 with leftovers

INGREDIENTS

1/2 cup red quinoa

1/2 cup Marinated Feta Cheese *(See recipe below.)*

1 cup Marinated Carrots *(See recipe below.)*

3/4 cup sugar snap peas, *snapped and cut on the bias*

2 cups Marinated Golden Beets *(See recipe below.)*

1 cup Marinated Chickpeas *(See recipe below.)*

2 farm eggs

2 ripe avocados

Salt and pepper to taste

Sherry Vinaigrette *(See recipe below.)*

2 cups mixed lettuce leaves

1/2 cup radish, *shaved*

Marinated Feta:

1/4 teaspoon cumin, *toasted and ground*

1/4 teaspoon of caraway seed, *toasted and ground*

1/2 teaspoon pink peppercorn, *ground*

1/2 cup (10 ounces) crumbled feta cheese

Marinated Carrots:

1 cup carrots

1 1/2 tablespoons sherry vinegar

Marinated Golden Beets:

1 1/2 pounds golden beets

1 bay leaf

1 chili de Arbol

3 thyme sprigs

1/2 cup white wine vinegar

1 1/2 cups water

Salt and pepper to taste

Marinated Chickpeas:

1/4 cup red onion, *small diced*

1/2 cup red bell pepper, *small diced*

1/2 cup sherry vinegar

3/4 cup canned garbanzo beans, *rinsed*

Sherry Vinaigrette:

1/4 cup sherry vinegar

1 shallot, minced

1/2 teaspoon thyme

1 teaspoon Dijon mustard

Salt and pepper to taste

3/4 cup grape seed oil

BOTTEGA BOWL

(continued)

DIRECTIONS:

For the quinoa: Bring a medium pot of lightly salted water to a boil. Drop quinoa in boiling water for 10-12 minutes until tender. Strain and reserve.

For the Marinated Feta: Combine all spices and toss with the crumbled feta. Set aside.

For the Marinated Carrots: Spiral cut the carrots; toss with sherry vinegar. Set aside.

For the sugar snap peas: Blanch the beans by boiling in salted water just until tender. Immediately immerse in an ice bath to preserve the color. Strain and set aside.

For the Marinated Beets: Place all items in a small sheet pan; cover with foil and roast in a 325° Fahrenheit oven for 30-45 minutes until tender. Remove beets from pan. Use towel to rub skin off, and then medium dice the beets.

For the Marinated Chickpeas: Combine all ingredients and let marinate for 30 minutes.

For the eggs: Bring a pot of water to a boil. Drop the eggs in the water for 10 minutes then submerge in ice water. Peel the eggs and cut in half. Season with salt and pepper.

For the avocado: Cut avocado in half; scoop out the flesh and cut into thirds. Season with salt and pepper.

For the Sherry Vinaigrette: Combine sherry vinegar, shallots, thyme, mustard, and salt and pepper in a bowl. Slowly whisk in the grape seed oil until incorporated.

To assemble: Divide the following ingredients evenly between 4 servings. Lightly dress the greens with the sherry vinaigrette and salt and pepper to taste; place in the bottom of the bowl. Place the quinoa in the center of bowl atop lettuce. Starting clockwise, add the marinated feta, marinated carrots, sugar snaps peas, marinated beets, shaved radish, marinated chickpeas, farm eggs, and avocado slices.

Post Office Pies Brussels Sprout & Kale Salad

POST OFFICE PIES

209 41st Street South
Birmingham, Alabama 35222
205-599-9900 | PostOfficePies.com

ESTABLISHED: 2014

KNOWN FOR: A quirky former post office location and Chef John Hall's hand-tossed, wood-fired pies crafted with the freshest local ingredients and cheeses. Sandwiched between Avondale Brewery and Saw's Soul Kitchen, partners Brandon Cain and Mike Wilson (of Saw's BBQ fame) teamed up with Hall on Post Office Pies, named one of The 33 Best Pizza Restaurants in the Country by Thrillist.com. Post Office Pies has a following for their salads almost as much as the pizza. The Brussels Sprout & Kale Salad boasts Brussels sprout hearts, fresh kale, smoked bacon, crushed red pepper, mint, and red wine vinaigrette. After begging for three years, we finally scored the recipe.

DON'T MISS: The house-made meatballs, tender and delicate but hearty, just like your Italian grandmother (if you had one) used to make. The stuffed breads are also not to be missed. The Jalapeño Cheese Bread or the Pepperoni Chunk Cheese Bread plus one of the signature salads makes the perfect lunch.

AVONDALE

POST OFFICE PIES BRUSSELS SPROUT and KALE SALAD

Yield: Serves 2-4, depending on portion size

INGREDIENTS

1/4 cup Brussels sprout hearts

1 quart Brussels leaves and kale mix

1/2 tablespoon canola oil

Salt and pepper to taste

1/4 cup bacon, *cooked and chopped*

2 mint leaves, *torn*

6 cilantro leaves, *torn*

Red Wine Vinaigrette, to taste *(Use homemade or store-bought.)*

1 teaspoon crushed red chili flakes for garnish

DIRECTIONS:

Preheat oven to 420° Fahrenheit.

Cut the root end off the Brussels sprouts. Peel off the outer leaves, excluding any discolored or bruised leaves, and place in a bowl and set aside.

Destem all kale, and rough chop or tear it into golf ball-size pieces. Then, wash and dry the pieces in a salad spinner. Mix the Brussels sprout leaves with the kale.

Cut the Brussels sprout hearts into quarters, toss in canola oil, and season with salt and pepper. Place on a sheet tray and roast in the oven for 12 minutes or until browned and tender. Set aside.

To assemble: In a large bowl, gently toss all ingredients together except the red chili flakes. Sprinkle chili flakes over the top before serving.

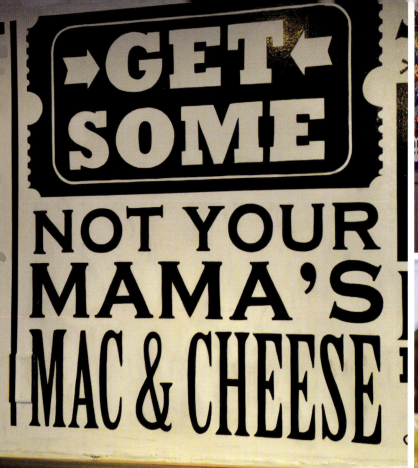

JOHN'S CITY DINER

112 Richard Arrington Jr. Boulevard North
Birmingham, Alabama 35203
205-322-6014 | JohnsCityDiner.com

ESTABLISHED: The original John's Restaurant, owned and made a local legend by John Proferis, the late father of Zoës Kitchen founder Zoë Cassimus, opened in 1944. The current owners, Shannon and Shana Gober, bought it in 2004.

KNOWN FOR: The trout. The original John's was known for Trout Almandine, and people still talk about it. The Gobers' modern version of that classic is their Parmesan Crusted Trout served over Roasted Corn Grits. The meatloaf is another revised classic dressed with red wine mushroom gravy and topped with fried onions.

DON'T MISS: The Crispy Duck. John's City Diner is one of the few places in town serving duck, and they do a fantastic job with it. Try the Good People Brewing beer-crusted Fish and Chips or the award-winning Three Little Pigs Macaroni & Cheese; both are comfort food favorites with John's unique spin.

Not Your Mama's Macaroni & Cheese

NOT YOUR MAMA'S MACARONI and CHEESE (The Original)

Yield: Serves 4-6, depending on portion size

INGREDIENTS

1 cup Japanese Panko breadcrumbs

1 (4-ounce) package thinly sliced prosciutto

1 (16-ounce) package penne pasta

1/2 cup unsalted butter

1 shallot, *minced*

1/4 cup dry white wine

1/4 cup all-purpose flour

2 cups whole milk *(You can substitute 2% or non-fat, but the taste will be different.)*

2 cups heavy cream or whipping cream

1 bay leaf

1/2 teaspoon salt

1/4 teaspoon ground red pepper

2 (10-ounce) blocks sharp white Cheddar cheese, *shredded*

1 cup shredded and divided smoked Gouda cheese *(You may substitute regular Gouda.)*

1/2 cup shredded Parmesan cheese

DIRECTIONS:

Preheat oven to 400° Fahrenheit.

Toast breadcrumbs in a single layer on a baking sheet 5-7 minutes or until golden, stirring once after 2 1/2 minutes. Set aside.

Cook prosciutto in batches in a lightly greased large skillet over medium heat 3-4 minutes on each side or until crisp. Drain on paper towels. Crumble. Set aside.

Prepare pasta according to package directions. Drain. Set aside.

Melt butter in a Dutch oven over medium heat; add shallot and sauté 3 minutes or until tender. Add wine, stirring to loosen particles from bottom of Dutch oven, and cook 1 minute more.

Gradually whisk in flour until smooth; cook, whisking constantly for 2 minutes. Gradually whisk in the milk and the next 4 ingredients. Cook, whisking constantly, 12-14 minutes or until mixture thickens and begins to bubble. Remove and discard bay leaf.

Place 4 cups cheddar cheese in a large, heatproof bowl. (You may have some cheddar cheese left. If so, keep it for a later use.) Add Gouda and Parmesan cheeses to bowl.

Gradually pour sauce over cheeses, whisking until cheeses are melted and sauce is smooth.

Stir in pasta and prosciutto until blended. Pour into a lightly greased 13x9-inch baking dish; sprinkle with the toasted breadcrumbs.

Bake at 400° for 15 minutes or until golden brown and bubbly. Serve immediately.

Note: Don't use pre-shredded cheese; it doesn't melt as smoothly. You can shred the cheese and crisp the prosciutto up to 1 day ahead and chill. You can also toast the breadcrumbs ahead and store them in a zip-top plastic bag until you are ready to use them.

Chef Chris Hastings, Hot and Hot Tomato Salad

HOT AND HOT FISH CLUB

Chef Chris Hastings, James Beard Award Winner

2180 11th Court South
Birmingham, Alabama 35205
205-933-5474 | HotAndHotFishClub.com

ESTABLISHED: 1995

KNOWN FOR: Modern, upscale Southern cuisine, steeped in tradition using locally sourced ingredients. Husband-wife team Chris and Idie Hastings opened the highly acclaimed Hot and Hot Fish Club in the historic Upside Down Plaza location in 1995 with a locally inspired menu that merges French, Southern, and California cuisines. The Hot and Hot Tomato Salad is so popular that fans wait all spring for the email announcing its return to the menu.

DON'T MISS: The chef's counter. It's a great place to watch the action in the open concept kitchen and learn some skills to improve your own cooking game. You cannot go wrong with the fish and the Iron Chef Rabbit Roulade that helped Chef Hastings slay Bobby Flay on Iron Chef America on the Food Network. The Country Captain, Hastings' spin on the old Southern classic curried chicken and rice stew, is fantastic. Order the soufflé for dessert when you walk in the door; it takes 30 minutes to prepare. Also note the beautiful Leeds, Alabama, Earthborn Pottery Chef Hastings uses for plating.

HOT and HOT TOMATO SALAD

Yield: Serves 6

INGREDIENTS

Balsamic Vinaigrette:

1/2 cup extra-virgin olive oil

1/2 cup olive oil

1 cup fresh chives, *finely chopped*

1 cup balsamic vinegar

1/2 cup green onions, *chopped*

1/4 teaspoon kosher salt

1/8 teaspoon freshly ground black pepper

Salad:

6 large beefsteak tomatoes

2 large golden delight tomatoes

2 large rainbow tomatoes

3/4 cup plus 3 tablespoons Balsamic Vinaigrette *(See recipe above.)*, *divided*

1 1/2 teaspoons kosher salt

3/4 teaspoon freshly ground black pepper

1 smoked ham hock

1 large onion, *peeled and quartered*

1 fresh thyme sprig

1 cup fresh field peas such as black-eye, pink-eye, Crowder, or butter beans

3 ears yellow corn, *husked*

2 tablespoons peanut oil

1/2 pint sweet 100 tomatoes *(Tiny currant tomatoes may be substituted.)*

Fried Okra *(See recipe right.)*

6 slices Applewood smoked bacon, *cooked until crisp*

3/4 cup Chive Dressing *(See recipe below.)*

6 tablespoons fresh basil, *chiffonade*

Fried Okra:

4 cups vegetable oil

30 pieces whole baby okra

1/4 cup whole-milk buttermilk

1/4 cup corn flour

1/4 cup corn meal

1/4 cup all-purpose flour

1 teaspoon kosher salt, *divided*

1/2 teaspoon freshly ground black pepper, *divided*

Chive Dressing:

1 small garlic clove, *peeled and finely minced*

6 tablespoons fresh chives, *finely chopped*

1 large egg yolk

2 tablespoons fresh lemon juice

1/2 teaspoon kosher salt

1/4 teaspoon freshly ground black pepper

1 cup olive oil

1/4 cup homemade Crème Fraîche *(or store bought)*

SOUTHSIDE

SOUTHSIDE

HOT and HOT TOMATO SALAD

(continued)

DIRECTIONS:

For the Balsamic Vinaigrette: Whisk together all of the ingredients in a large bowl. The vinaigrette can be used immediately or stored in an airtight container in the refrigerator for up to 5 days. Be sure to bring the chilled vinaigrette to room temperature and whisk well before serving. Makes 2 cups.

For the salad: Core and slice beefsteak, golden delight, and rainbow tomatoes into 1/4-inch thick slices. Toss the tomatoes with 3/4 cup vinaigrette. Season the tomatoes with salt and pepper and set aside at room temperature to marinate until ready to serve.

Combine the ham hock, onion, thyme, and field peas in a medium stockpot with enough cold water to cover the beans. Bring the peas to a simmer and cook until just tender, 12 to 15 minutes, stirring occasionally. Remove from the heat, drain, and cool. Remove and discard the ham hock, onion quarters, and thyme sprig. Place the cooled peas in a mixing bowl and set aside.

Shave the kernels off the corn cobs, discarding the silk hairs. Heat the peanut oil in a large skillet over medium-high heat. Add the corn kernels and cook until tender, 8 to 10 minutes. Season the corn with salt and pepper to taste, and remove from the heat and cool slightly. Toss the corn kernels with the cooked field peas and the remaining 3 tablespoons of vinaigrette. Set the pea mixture aside to marinate at room temperature until ready to serve.

For the okra: Pour the vegetable oil into a deep-sided skillet to a depth of 3 inches. (Alternately, a deep fryer can be filled with vegetable oil.) Preheat the oil to 350° Fahrenheit.

Trim the okra stems and place okra pods in a small bowl with the buttermilk. Toss until well coated.

Combine the corn flour, cornmeal, all-purpose flour, salt, and pepper in medium size bowl. Drain the okra from the buttermilk and toss in the cornmeal mixture. Shake off any excess cornmeal mixture. Place the okra in the preheated vegetable oil and fry for 2-3 minutes or until golden. Remove okra from the hot oil with a slotted spoon and drain on a paper towel-lined plate. Season the okra with the remaining salt and pepper if needed. Keep warm until ready to serve.

For the Chive Dressing: Combine the garlic and chives in a small bowl. Add egg yolk, lemon juice, salt, and pepper, and whisk to combine. Add the olive oil in a thin, steady stream while whisking vigorously. This should create an emulsion. Whisk in the Crème Fraîche. You may need to add a drop or two of water if dressing is too thick. Cover and chill the dressing for at least 20 minutes before serving. This dressing will keep refrigerated in an airtight container for up to two days. Makes about 1 1/4 cups.

To serve: Arrange each of the different types of sliced tomatoes on six plates. Place the whole sweet 100 tomatoes around the sliced tomatoes. Divide the pea and corn mixture evenly among plates on top of the tomatoes. Arrange 5 pieces of fried okra around each plate and place 1 slice of crispy bacon on the top of each salad. Drizzle 1-2 tablespoons Chive Dressing over the tops of each salad and garnish each with 1 tablespoon basil. Serve immediately.

Recipe copyright Chef Chris Hastings

OVENBIRD

Chef Chris Hastings, James Beard Award Winner

2810 3rd Avenue South
Birmingham, Alabama 35233
205-957-6686 | OvenbirdRestaurant.com

ESTABLISHED: 2015

KNOWN FOR: Live-fire cooking starring locally sourced seasonal Southern and many unusual ingredients from farm and field, land and air, ocean and estuaries, and orchards and dairies. The husband and wife team of Chris and Idie Hastings has created a casual, romantic garden dining experience nestled in the crepe myrtles found in Charlie Thigpen's Garden Gallery at Pepper Place. The menu reveals influences from the South as well as Spain and South America. Seasonal cocktails are paired with the menu, and the small plate format makes it possible to sample a variety of dishes.

DON'T MISS: The Empanadas (Argentine meat pies) or the Beef Fat Candle, which is beef, sofrito, and jus served with a beef fat tea light candle. Play it safe with the Spit-Roasted Chicken, which is unlike any other in town, or try something really different like the Braised Goat with soft-poached egg, grits, and preserved lemon. Its extremely popular Humitas is similar to grits in consistency but made with fresh corn and topped with a wood-fire charred salsa. Serve it as a side dish with your favorite meat, poultry, or fish. The salsa on its own is a wonderful accompaniment to any grilled food.

Humitas with Charred Herb Salsa. Photo: Courtesy of Ovenbird

OVENBIRD HUMITAS with CHARRED HERB SALSA
(Creamy Corn with Charred Herb Salsa)

Yield: Serves 10-12, depending on portion size

INGREDIENTS

Humitas:

16 ears fresh corn

1/2 cup unsalted butter

1/4 cup extra-virgin olive oil

4 cups yellow onion, *chopped*

2 cups milk

Salt and pepper to taste

1 1/4 tablespoons red pepper flakes

Basil for garnish

Charred Herb Salsa:

1 bunch parsley plus additional 1/2 cup, *minced*

1 bunch thyme

1 bunch oregano

3 sprigs fennel frond

3 cloves garlic, *minced*

4 sprigs mint, *minced*

6 garlic scapes (if available), *chopped*

2 dried chili peppers, *minced*

1 cup red wine vinegar

1 cup extra-virgin olive oil

Zest from 1/2 lemon

Salt and pepper to taste

DIRECTIONS:

For the Humitas: Grate corn using the largest setting on the box grater. Using the back of a knife, scrape the remaining liquid and corn from the cob. Melt butter and olive oil in a Dutch oven over medium heat. Add onions and sauté until translucent. Stir in corn with all the liquid until it thickens. Stir in milk and reduce until it thickens. Season with salt and pepper and pepper flakes, and add basil.

For the salsa: Combine the parsley, thyme, oregano, and fennel frond and tie in a bundle. Grill over wood until slightly charred on the outside on all sides. Untie and remove stems, chop fine. Add to a bowl and combine with the rest of the ingredients.

IRONDALE CAFE

1906 1st Avenue North
Irondale, Alabama 35210
205-956-5258 | IrondaleCafe.com

ESTABLISHED: 1928

KNOWN FOR: Fried Green Tomatoes, made famous by the Fannie Flagg movie and book of the same name. Owner Jim Dolan and his crew serve 600-800 slices of their signature dish every day. If you don't go over the tracks to "The Original Whistle Stop Café" for the fried green tomatoes, go for the meat-and-three and homemade desserts.

DON'T MISS: The buttermilk fried chicken and the chicken and dumplings that have had people standing in line since the restaurant opened. Fans drive to Irondale specifically for the fried chicken livers, and others swear the macaroni and cheese is better than their mama's. Many folks go just for the fresh veggies and cornbread. The desserts have legions of fans as well. Try the Buttermilk Pie, a house specialty. Don't forget the endless glass of cold sweet tea to go with your meal; it will always be refilled with a smile.

Fried Green Tomatoes

IRONDALE

IRONDALE CAFÉ'S FAMOUS FRIED GREEN TOMATOES

Yield: 12 tomato slices

INGREDIENTS

1 1/4 cups cream meal*

3/4 cup corn flour*

1 cup self-rising flour

1 1/2 cups whole buttermilk

1/2-3/4 cup water, *added a little at a time until desired consistency is reached*

Canola oil for frying

4 medium-size green tomatoes, *cut into 1/3-inch slices*

Salt and pepper to taste

DIRECTIONS:

Combine the first 5 ingredients in a bowl and stir until smooth and lump free. Set aside.

Pour the frying oil into the skillet to a depth of about 1/2 inch and heat to 320° Fahrenheit.

Coat both sides of the tomato slices in the batter mixture, and tap to remove the excess batter. Fry slices on both sides until golden brown. (Note: Do not overcrowd the pan or the oil temperature will drop and result in a soggy exterior.) Drain slices on a paper towel for 10 seconds. Season with salt and pepper. Serve.

*You can find cream meal and corn flour online and in most organic grocery stores in the flour aisle. The Bob's Red Mill brand was used for this recipe.

Baby Blue Salad

HOMEWOOD GOURMET

1919 28th Avenue South, Suite 113
Homewood, Alabama 35209
205-871-1620 | HomewoodGourmet.com

ESTABLISHED: 1996

KNOWN FOR: Creative, healthy food with New Orleans flare by the husband and wife chef-owner team Laura and Chris Zapalowski, who settled in Birmingham after their evacuation during Hurricane Katrina. Their popular Dinner in a Dash meals feed up to four people. The Baby Blue Salad, made famous by the original owner, Chef Franklin Biggs, is one of their most requested recipes.

DON'T MISS: The Jambalaya, Red Beans and Rice, and other New Orleans favorites. The Chicken Pot Pie, a Monday special, is one you have to try. The Bread Pudding is one of the best in town. If you have a chance, take one of their cooking classes!

BABY BLUE SALAD

Yield: Serves 2-4, depending on portion size

INGREDIENTS

Spiced Pecans:

1/4 cup plus 2 tablespoons sugar, *divided*

1 cup warm water

1 cup pecan halves

1 tablespoon chili powder

1/8 teaspoon ground red pepper

Dressing:

1/2 cup balsamic vinegar

3 tablespoons Dijon mustard

3 tablespoons honey

1 tablespoon chopped fresh garlic

1 tablespoon chopped fresh shallots

1 1/2 cups olive oil

1/2 teaspoon salt

1/4 teaspoon ground pepper

Salad:

1 (5-ounce) bag mixed spring salad greens

1/4 cup crumbled blue cheese

1 orange, *peeled and sectioned*

1/2 pint fresh strawberries, *hulled and quartered*

DIRECTIONS:

Preheat oven to 350° Fahrenheit.

For the Spiced Pecans: Stir together 1/4 cup sugar and warm water until sugar dissolves. Add pecans; soak 10 minutes. Drain and discard liquid.

Combine remaining 2 tablespoons sugar, chili powder, and red pepper. Add pecans; toss to coat. Place pecans in a single layer on a lightly greased baking sheet. Bake at 350° for 10 minutes or until golden brown, stirring once. Set aside to cool. (Note: Leftovers will keep for several weeks in an airtight container.)

For the dressing: Whisk the vinegar, Dijon, honey, garlic, and shallots together in a large mixing bowl. Slowly drizzle in the oil while whisking constantly. Season with salt and pepper. Set aside until ready to use.

To serve: Toss together salad greens, blue cheese, orange segments, and strawberries in a large bowl. Drizzle with 1/3-1/2 cup dressing, gently tossing to coat. Reserve remaining vinaigrette for another use. Top salad with 1/2 cup spiced pecans, and serve immediately.

Ashley Mac's

ASHLEY MAC'S CAFE | CATERING | GOURMET-TO-GO

Cahaba Heights
3147 Green Valley Road
Cahaba Heights, Alabama 35243
205-822-4142 | AshleyMacs.com

Inverness
5299 Valleydale Road
Hoover, Alabama 35242
205-822-4142 | AshleyMacs.com

Riverchase
4730 Chace Circle, #100
Hoover, Alabama 35244
205-259-5044 | AshleyMacs.com

ESTABLISHED: 2007

KNOWN FOR: Ashley Mac's famous strawberry cake, the best seller and the signature recipe that helped build the brand. What started as a love of cooking turned into a successful home-based catering operation that rapidly bloomed into three restaurants. Ashley's salads are very popular for lunch, and its spinach salad recipe was the most requested since it is not always on the menu.

DON'T MISS: The meals to-go. After lunch, head over to the freezer and stock up on Ashley Mac's homemade frozen favorites for dinner. They are perfect for those hectic nights during the week when there's no time to cook. The BBQ Meatloaf and Chicken Pot Pie are two of the most popular. The new Caramel Cake and cupcakes are the most recent introductions.

Spinach Salad with Dijon Vinaigrette Dressing

ASHLEY MAC'S SPINACH SALAD with DIJON VINAIGRETTE DRESSING

Yield: Serves 8-10 with 2 cups of Dijon Vinaigrette

INGREDIENTS

Salad:

9 ounces fresh spinach

1 1/2 avocado, *diced*

3 tablespoons Craisins®

3 tablespoons feta cheese

3 tablespoons almonds slivers or pecan halves, *toasted*

1/2 red onion, *thinly sliced*

Dijon Vinaigrette:

1 tablespoon Dijon mustard

1/2 cup apple cider vinegar

1 cup olive oil

1/4 cup granulated sugar

1/2 teaspoon salt

1/2 teaspoon ground black pepper

1 teaspoon Italian seasoning

DIRECTIONS:

For the salad: Place spinach in bowl and top with remaining ingredients.

For the Dijon Vinaigrette: Whisk together the Dijon, vinegar, and sugar. Slowly stream in the olive oil, whisking as you pour. Stir in salt, pepper, and Italian seasoning.

Toss the salad with the dressing and serve.

Note: The dressing may be chilled before use but should be served at room temperature. Excess will keep for 1 week in the refrigerator.

CAHABA HEIGHTS, INVERNESS, AND RIVERCHASE

Notes

Zoës Kitchen Live Med Salad

ZOËS KITCHEN

The Summit | Inverness | Crestline Village
Homewood | Downtown | Vestavia Hills
ZoesKitchen.com

ESTABLISHED: 1995

KNOWN FOR: Fast, fresh, casual Greek and Mediterranean food served with the same Southern hospitality the chain was founded upon by its original owners, Birmingham's Cassimus family. Zoë, Marcus, and John Cassimus took the family's recipes and turned them into what would become one of America's first and most successful "fast-casual" dining concepts. Although the chain has been purchased and the corporate offices are no longer based in Birmingham, Zoës Kitchen will always be a favorite of locals who remember standing in line at the original Homewood location to get an order of Chicken Roll-Ups, a Greek Salad, or Zoë's famous Chicken and Orzo Soup.

DON'T MISS: The Gruben, Zoës' healthy spin on a Reuben. Other favorites are the Protein Power Plate or the Chicken Salad and Fruit Plate. If you have a sweet craving, get the chocolate cake; it is still made with the grainy old-school fudge icing the way Zoë's mother made it back in the day. The Limeade is still squeezed by hand, and like the chocolate cake, it has been on the menu since day one.

ZOËS KITCHEN LIVE MED SALAD

Yield: 2 dinner portion salads or 4 side salad portions

INGREDIENTS

Pesto Farro:

1 1/2 cup farro

1/2 cup roasted tomatoes, *chopped (You may use canned or roast your own.)*

2 tablespoons basil pesto *(store-bought or homemade)*

1 teaspoon lemon juice

1 teaspoon extra-virgin olive oil

Salad:

1 cup fresh spinach

1 cup zucchini, *sliced into ribbons*

1 cup yellow squash, *sliced into ribbons*

1/4 cup red onion, *diced*

1/4 cup red cherry tomatoes, *halved*

1/4 cup yellow cherry tomatoes, *halved*

1 tablespoon basil, *diced*

1/4 cup lupini beans, *brined and deshelled (You may find canned at Whole Foods, but the dry version must be soaked overnight.)*

Your favorite vinaigrette *(Zoës uses their Calabrian Pepper Vinaigrette.)*

1 tablespoon grated Parmesan

DIRECTIONS:

For the Pesto Farro: Bring 4 cups of lightly salted water to a boil; add 1 cup farro. Cook for approximately 16 minutes or until al dente; drain, then cool. Combine all ingredients for Pesto Farro in a mixing bowl and mix gently until fully incorporated.

For the salad: Combine spinach, zucchini, squash, red onions, tomatoes, basil, and vinaigrette in a mixing bowl and toss together. Transfer onto serving plate and sprinkle Parmesan evenly over the salad. Place the Pesto Farro in the center. Spread lupini beans evenly around the outside of the salad.

Soups & Sandwiches

Dyron's Lowcountry
▶▶ Seafood Gumbo 128

Holler & Dash
▶▶ Kickback Chicken 130

Sol's Sandwich Shop & Deli
▶▶ Super Sol Burger 132

Formosa Hoover Chinese Restaurant
▶▶ Hot and Sour Soup 134

Gilchrist Sandwich Shop
▶▶ Hot Beef Sandwich 136

5 Point Public House
▶▶ George's Oyster Stew 138

Revelator Coffee
▶▶ Everything Toast 140

Brick & Tin
▶▶ Butternut Squash Soup 142

Busy Corner Cheese & Provisions
▶▶ The Augusta 144

Snapper Grabber's Coastal Kitchen
▶▶ Baja Shrimp Tacos 146

Shindig's Catering & Food Truck
▶▶ Grass-Fed Beef Willis Burger 148

DYRON'S LOWCOUNTRY

121 Oak Street
Mountain Brook, Alabama 35213
205-834-8257 | DyronsLowcountry.com

ESTABLISHED: 2009

KNOWN FOR: Steaks, rich braises, and Lowcountry cuisine as found in the coastal regions of South Carolina and Georgia. Dyron's seafood gumbo even has a fan club; regular customers demand it, even when it is hot outside. The dark roux takes 3-4 hours to cook, and it is loaded with Gulf lump crabmeat and whole shrimp.

DON'T MISS: She-Crab Soup when it is in season. The ribeye is one of the best in town, and if short ribs happen to be on the menu when you visit, order them. The back room is casual and great for watching the game with friends. Sunday brunch is one of the best in town.

Dyron's Seafood Gumbo

CRESTLINE VILLAGE

DYRON'S SEAFOOD GUMBO

Yield: 6-8 bowls or 12-16 cups, depending on portion size

INGREDIENTS

2 sticks unsalted butter

1 cup all-purpose flour

Olive oil

4 cloves garlic, *peeled and crushed*

1 red bell pepper, *diced small*

1 green bell pepper, *diced small*

2 yellow onions, *diced small*

4 stalks celery, *diced small*

1 bunch fresh thyme, *tied with kitchen twine*

3 bay leaves

Salt and pepper to taste

1 quart skinless whole Centro brand San Marzano tomatoes, *crushed*

1 1/2 tablespoon gumbo filè *(Find in the spice aisle.)*

1 1/2 tablespoons olive oil

3 quarts fish stock

Tabasco to taste

3 tablespoons Worcestershire sauce

1 (12-ounce) Budweiser beer, *at room temperature*

Cooked rice *(Use your favorite basmati or jasmine rice, cooked according to package directions.)*

1 pound (about 36) Gulf shrimp, *cooked and peeled*

1 pound jumbo lump crabmeat *(Purchase pre-cooked.)*

DIRECTIONS:

Preheat oven to 325° Fahrenheit.

For the roux: In a large ovenproof skillet or Dutch oven, combine flour and butter on medium heat until the roux is blonde or light caramel in color. Place in the oven and cook for 3-4 hours or until dark chocolate brown, stirring every 15 minutes. Set aside.

For the gumbo: Generously coat the bottom of a heavy stockpot with the olive oil and preheat on medium heat. Add the garlic and sauté until golden. Add in the peppers, onions, celery, thyme, and bay leaves. Sauté with a little salt until tender. Add tomatoes and file. Add roux, stirring with a wooden spoon until smooth. Add the fish stock, a few shakes of Tabasco, and a generous amount of Worcestershire followed by the beer. Salt and pepper to taste. Simmer for 45 minutes to 1 hour, stirring every few minutes.

To plate: Add the desired amount of cooked rice, shrimp, and lump crabmeat to each bowl. Spoon hot gumbo over the top. The addition of the seafood and rice when the gumbo is plated keeps the seafood from becoming overcooked and the rice from getting mushy.

HOLLER & DASH

2801 18th Street South
Homewood, Alabama 35209
205-414-0999 | HollerAndDash.com

ESTABLISHED: 2016

KNOWN FOR: Southern-style buttermilk biscuits in all sorts of delicious configurations for breakfast, brunch, and lunch. Featuring a chef-driven menu with local and regionally sourced ingredients, it is the newest of the fast casual restaurant chains to have originated in Birmingham. Part of the Cracker Barrel family, Holler & Dash is rapidly growing with locations in Tuscaloosa as well as Celebration, Florida, and Brentwood, Tennessee.

DON'T MISS: The Grit Bowl featuring Shelby County's famous McEwen & Sons stone ground grits topped with a fried egg. Try the Tot Bowl, a bowl of crispy tater tots with bacon, cheese, and green onions, or the open-face Andouille Hustle biscuit. For a sweeter option, order the Strawberry and Dash, their spin on a Belgian Waffle with whipped Creole cream cheese, and strawberries dusted with powdered sugar.

Kickback Chicken

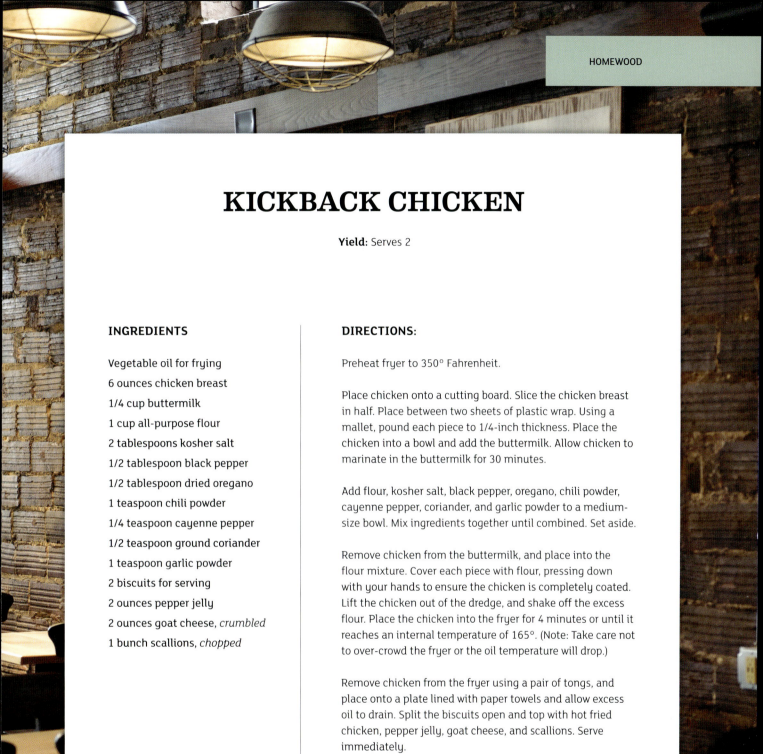

HOMEWOOD

KICKBACK CHICKEN

Yield: Serves 2

INGREDIENTS

Vegetable oil for frying
6 ounces chicken breast
1/4 cup buttermilk
1 cup all-purpose flour
2 tablespoons kosher salt
1/2 tablespoon black pepper
1/2 tablespoon dried oregano
1 teaspoon chili powder
1/4 teaspoon cayenne pepper
1/2 teaspoon ground coriander
1 teaspoon garlic powder
2 biscuits for serving
2 ounces pepper jelly
2 ounces goat cheese, *crumbled*
1 bunch scallions, *chopped*

DIRECTIONS:

Preheat fryer to 350° Fahrenheit.

Place chicken onto a cutting board. Slice the chicken breast in half. Place between two sheets of plastic wrap. Using a mallet, pound each piece to 1/4-inch thickness. Place the chicken into a bowl and add the buttermilk. Allow chicken to marinate in the buttermilk for 30 minutes.

Add flour, kosher salt, black pepper, oregano, chili powder, cayenne pepper, coriander, and garlic powder to a medium-size bowl. Mix ingredients together until combined. Set aside.

Remove chicken from the buttermilk, and place into the flour mixture. Cover each piece with flour, pressing down with your hands to ensure the chicken is completely coated. Lift the chicken out of the dredge, and shake off the excess flour. Place the chicken into the fryer for 4 minutes or until it reaches an internal temperature of 165°. (Note: Take care not to over-crowd the fryer or the oil temperature will drop.)

Remove chicken from the fryer using a pair of tongs, and place onto a plate lined with paper towels and allow excess oil to drain. Split the biscuits open and top with hot fried chicken, pepper jelly, goat cheese, and scallions. Serve immediately.

Super Sol Burger

SOL'S SANDWICH SHOP & DELI

2 20th Street North, Suite 120
Birmingham, Alabama 35203
205-244-7657 | SolsDeli.com

ESTABLISHED: Original Sol's 1968, Reopened 2007

KNOWN FOR: Its burgers, sandwiches, and comfort food favorites. A Birmingham tradition came back to life when brothers Jeff, Chris, and Jason Bajalieh opened Sol's Sandwich Shop and Deli to honor their late father, Sol, who opened the original Sol's in downtown Birmingham. Lunchtime crowds flock to Sol's for their house-ground burgers and daily specials. Mama Bajalieh makes a mean meatloaf!

DON'T MISS: The Super Sol Burger and the Camel Rider, a house-ground beef burger in a pita pocket, are Sol's most popular orders. Fans claim Sol's has the city's best breakfast. The Magic City Omelet with jack cheese and the breakfast sandwiches (get one to-go) are big favorites with the downtown crowd. When Baked Greek Chicken or Stuffed Grape Leaves are on the menu, go early because they go fast!

DOWNTOWN

SUPER SOL BURGER

Yield: 4 (1/4-pound) burgers

INGREDIENTS

1 pound ground beef

1 teaspoon kosher salt

1 teaspoon ground black pepper

4 slices American cheese

4 hamburger buns

Mayonnaise

Yellow mustard

Ketchup

Lettuce

Pickles

4 thick slices tomato

Onion

DIRECTIONS:

In a bowl, mix the ground beef, salt, and pepper until well blended. Divide mixture into four equal portions and shape each into a patty about 4 inches wide.

Lay patties on hot griddle or in a cast iron skillet. Cook burgers until browned on both sides and no longer pink inside, approximately 7 to 8 minutes. Remove from the heat.

Lay buns, cut side down, on griddle until lightly toasted, about 30 seconds-1 minute. Add a slice of cheese to the top bun and spread mayonnaise, mustard, and ketchup on bun bottoms. Stack bun with lettuce, pickles, tomato, burger, onion, and salt and pepper to taste. Set bun tops in place and serve.

Notes

FORMOSA HOOVER CHINESE RESTAURANT

2109 Lorna Ridge Drive
Hoover, Alabama 35216
205-900-8021

ESTABLISHED: 1983 in Five Points West, moved to Hoover in 1991, closed in 2012. Formosa reopened in 2016 to the delight of generations of loyal customers.

KNOWN FOR: Chinese cuisine and a family atmosphere. The one dish that all the regulars agree is the best they've ever had is Formosa's Hot and Sour Soup. Thankfully, Gary not only shared the recipe, but he also gave us a cooking lesson on how to make it. They use fresh ingredients and old-school cooking methods with recipes made the same way since 1983. Regulars highly recommend the Coconut Butter Chicken or the Coconut Butter Shrimp, dishes unique to Formosa.

DON'T MISS: The Sweet Corn Chicken Soup. The Lo Mein gets raves as does the Moo Shoo Pork. The Shredded Beef with Garlic Sauce has water chestnuts, green onions, mushrooms, and a special garlic sauce. Go for lunch if you find yourself in Hoover; the service is fast and the prices are very affordable. If you are an Egg Foo Young fan, the house version is fantastic.

Formosa Hot and Sour Soup

HOOVER

FORMOSA HOT and SOUR SOUP

Yield: Serves 4-6, depending on portion size

INGREDIENTS

1 dried Chinese mushroom like Woodear

1 tablespoon sesame oil

4 shrimp

4 scallops

3 ounces chicken

4 cups homemade chicken broth *(or substitute store-bought)*

1 cup soy sauce

3 cups medium-sized white button mushrooms, *sliced thin*

1/4 cup firm water-packed tofu, *drained and cut into cubes*

3 teaspoons white pepper

1 1/2 tablespoons potato starch *(Find in the baking aisle by the cornstarch.)*

1/2 cup warm water

1/4 cup bamboo shoots

3 eggs, *beaten*

1/2 cup white vinegar *(For best results, use vinegar with 4-5% acidity.)*

Green onions, *sliced diagonally, for garnish*

DIRECTIONS:

If you are using a dried Woodear mushroom, cover with 1 cup boiling water to reconstitute. Let stand for 30 minutes.

In a large wok, heat the oil over medium-high heat. Add shrimp, scallops, and chicken and stir-fry 2 minutes or until done. Add the mushroom and the water along with the next 5 ingredients. Bring to a boil, reduce heat, and simmer for 5 minutes.

Dissolve potato starch in the warm water and stir into the soup. Add the bamboo shoots. Increase the heat and bring to a boil. Reduce heat to medium and cook for 1 minute more. Gently swirl beaten eggs into the hot liquid. Add the vinegar. Cook for 1 minute over low heat. Remove from heat and serve sprinkled with sliced green onions for garnish.

GILCHRIST SANDWICH SHOP

2805 Cahaba Road
Birmingham, Alabama 35223
205-871-2181

ESTABLISHED: 1928

KNOWN FOR: Hand-scooped milkshakes and lunch counter favorites like homemade egg salad, BLT, and pimento cheese sandwiches. Grilled cheese and chili are popular in the cooler months. Be sure to order their fresh-squeezed limeade; it is on the list of 100 Things to Eat in Alabama Before You Die. Be sure to grab a seat at the counter; the green barstools have been there since the place opened. Some Mountain Brook families claim 4-5 generations have a favorite barstool or table at Gilchrist.

DON'T MISS: Tomato Aspic, a timeless Southern tradition that few places still serve. It has also been around since the shop's beginning and is still popular today. Don't skip the shake; almost everyone who has had one thinks a Gilchrist handspun milkshake is just the thing to cure whatever ails you. You can get them to-go, but they seem to taste so much better in a vintage ice cream soda glass so frosty that you'll leave fingerprints on the side of the glass.

Hot Beef Sandwich

MOUNTAIN BROOK VILLAGE

GILCHRIST HOT BEEF SANDWICH

Yield: 4 sandwiches

INGREDIENTS

1 pound ground beef

1/2 cup yellow onion, *diced*

1 tablespoon salt

1 tablespoon ground pepper

2 1/2 cups water

4 hamburger buns, *split and toasted*

Butter, *optional*

Mayonnaise

Mustard

Pickles for garnish, *optional*

Pimiento Cheese for garnish, *optional*

DIRECTIONS:

Add beef, onion, salt, pepper, and water to a large pot or saucepan. Bring to a boil, and as it cooks, break up the ground beef into fine pieces. Reduce the heat and simmer for at least 30 minutes. The longer you cook it, the better it is.

Before serving, split and toast the hamburger buns, using a little butter to toast them if you desire. Spread the buns with a little mayonnaise and mustard.

To serve: Strain the excess liquid from the beef. Put a scoop of the beef in the middle of the bun; add a couple of hamburger pickles or even a scoop of Pimento Cheese if you like and replace the top. Serve hot.

Notes

Photo: Oyster-Obsession.com

George's Oyster Stew

5 POINT PUBLIC HOUSE OYSTER BAR

1210 20th Street South
Birmingham, Alabama 35205
205-918-0726 | 5PointPublicHouse.com

ESTABLISHED: 2015

KNOWN FOR: Oysters and elevated pub fare. Chef George Reis has created a casual oyster haven next door to Ocean with one of the city's best selection of Alabama-farmed oysters like the highly rated Point aux Pins, Murder Point, and Isle Dauphine oysters, plus a daily offering of acclaimed oysters from around the United States. The bar snack menu and extensive craft beer selection have amassed a following as has the Poutine with garlic Parmesan fries, pulled pork, cheese curds, and beef gravy.

DON'T MISS: Oysters, of course. Pick a dozen raw on the half shell from the daily menu, and note the differences between the varieties. The fish and chips and the burgers are a must, and so is the Chicken and White Cheddar Biscuit (yes, at an oyster house).

GEORGE'S OYSTER STEW

Yield: Serves 3, depending on portion size

INGREDIENTS

2 tablespoons unsalted butter

1 1/2 tablespoons green onions, *chopped, plus more for garnish*

1 dozen large Gulf oysters with liquor intact *(or shucked Nelson Brothers Oysters from Bon Secour, Alabama)*

3 cups half-and-half

1/4 teaspoon salt

1/4 teaspoon white pepper

Cayenne pepper sauce to taste *(5 Point uses their own house-made sauce, but you may substitute Tabasco.)*

Hot biscuits or warm French bread for serving

DIRECTIONS:

Cook green onions over medium heat in melted butter. Add the oyster liquor, half-and-half, salt, and pepper. Heat to a simmer; do not boil. Add the oysters and cook until edges just begin to curl.

Add your favorite cayenne pepper sauce to taste.

Serve over hot biscuits or with a warm slice of French bread. Slice green onion over the top as garnish.

Notes

Revelator's Everything Toast

REVELATOR COFFEE

1826 3rd Avenue North, Unit 101
Birmingham, Alabama 35203
205-224-5900 | RevelatorCoffee.com

ESTABLISHED: 2014

KNOWN FOR: Craft coffee. Yes, the next big coffee trend is based in Birmingham and expanding rapidly across the Southeast. Fans love the modern and minimalist vibe that is all about the coffee. When Eater, *Southern Living*, and Thrillist are writing about your business, well, you must be doing something right.

DON'T MISS: The pour over coffee, a fan favorite. But the latte (hot or cold) with cinnamon and honey has a loyal following, too. Breakfast changes daily, but the Everything Toast with avocado has folks coming back again and again and was our most requested recipe. Support the Revelator team when you are on the road; you can now get your fix in New Orleans, Atlanta, Nashville, Charleston, or Chattanooga.

DOWNTOWN

REVELATOR'S EVERYTHING TOAST

Yield: 2 servings (You can half the ricotta spread recipe, if desired, or save the leftover in the fridge for another use.)

INGREDIENTS

Everything Ricotta Spread:

2 1/2 cups ricotta cheese (homemade or store bought)

1/2 cup dried minced onion

1/2 cup poppy seeds

1 cup sesame seeds

1/4 cup flake or kosher salt

Toast:

Sourdough bread

3 tablespoons Everything Ricotta Spread *(See recipe above.)*

2 ounces smoked salmon

1 cup arugula

1 tablespoon fresh squeezed lemon juice

DIRECTIONS:

For the ricotta spread: Add the ricotta cheese to a large bowl. Add dried minced onion, poppy seeds, sesame seeds, and salt. Stir until blended. Refrigerate and serve chilled. (Note: Toast the seeds in a dry pan if desired.)

To assemble: Cut thick slices of sourdough bread and lightly toast both sides. Generously spread 3 tablespoons of the ricotta spread onto each slice of toast. Layer with smoked salmon, arugula, and a spritz of lemon juice. Slice into three pieces. Serve.

Notes

BRICK & TIN

Mountain Brook Village
2901 Cahaba Road
Mountain Brook, Alabama 35223
205-502-7971 | BrickAndTin.com

Downtown
214 20th Street North
Birmingham, Alabama 35203
205-297-8636 | BrickAndTin.com

ESTABLISHED: Downtown 2010, Mountain Brook 2014

KNOWN FOR: Farm-to-fork, high-quality fast-casual dining with house-made artisanal breads and locally sourced ingredients from purveyors as close to home as possible. Seasonal cocktails are fashioned to complement the menu. Salads are ever changing, based on what the farmers are delivering that day.

DON'T MISS: The pastrami sandwich. They bake all of the bread (try the rosemary potato sourdough) for sandwiches and paninis each day and have a large selection of fresh baked cookies, pastries, and breads to purchase. Having a party? Order the bread pudding from the catering menu. Trust us.

Butternut Squash Soup

MOUNTAIN BROOK VILLAGE
AND DOWNTOWN

BUTTERNUT SQUASH SOUP

Yield: Serves 6

INGREDIENTS

1/4 pound unsalted butter

1 large yellow onion, *peeled and thinly sliced*

2 tablespoons kosher salt, *divided*

2 medium (1 large) butternut squash, *peeled, seeded, and cut into 2-inch cubes*

2 cups heavy whipping cream

Extra-virgin olive oil

Homemade Crème Fraiche:

Note: Requires 48 hours advance preparation

1 1/2 tablespoons whole buttermilk

1 cup whole milk

DIRECTIONS:

In a heavy pot, melt the butter over medium heat. Add the onions and season with 1 tablespoon kosher salt. Slowly sweat the onions over medium heat, stirring occasionally until they're completely soft, translucent, and very fragrant. There should be no browning or caramelization on the pot.

Add the butternut squash pieces and stir together with the onions. Continue to gently sauté for 5 minutes to begin to release the fragrance of the squash. Cover the vegetables with 1-2 inches of water. Add 1 tablespoon kosher salt. Turn the heat to high and bring the water to a simmer. Turn the heat down, and gently simmer until all the squash pieces can be easily mashed with a fork, about 15-20 minutes.

Carefully transfer the soup in small batches to a blender and puree until completely smooth or use an immersion blender instead. Be sure to start the blender slowly to avoid the hot liquid coming out the top. You may need to add a little more water to the blender if the mixture is too thick so that all of the squash is pureed. When the mixture is completely combined and smooth, add the heavy cream, whisking fully to combine. Season to taste with more salt as needed.

For the Crème Fraiche: Whisk the buttermilk and milk together and place in a glass container. Cover tightly and leave at room temperature for 48 hours. Whisk and refrigerate. It keeps for 5-7 days covered in the refrigerator.

To serve: Ladle the soup into a bowl and garnish with a drizzle of the olive oil and a dollop of Crème Fraiche.

The Augusta

BUSY CORNER CHEESE & PROVISIONS @ THE PIZITZ FOOD HALL

1821 2nd Ave North
Birmingham, Alabama 35203
205-730-1886 | BusyCornerCheese.com

ESTABLISHED: 2017

KNOWN FOR: Imported and domestic cheeses you just cannot find anywhere else in the city. The cheeses at Busy Corner are sourced and curated by owner and lead cheesemonger Brian McMillian, who spent the past 20 years on a quest for greater cheese knowledge as a chef and cheese importer. He brings cheeses directly from the makers and farmers to the Busy Corner, where the knowledgeable staff will help you with your selection and hand cut the amount you want.

DON'T MISS: The cheese and charcuterie boards and the sandwiches! Of course, Busy Corner Cheese has a fantastic selection of cheeses, cured meats, and other charcuterie staples, but while you're there, be sure to grab a sandwich, too. The Augusta, the most requested recipe, boasts melty pimento cheese with a green tomato relish.

DOWNTOWN

THE AUGUSTA

Yield: 10 sandwiches. You can half the recipe, if desired; the leftover pimento cheese will keep for at least a week in the refrigerator.

INGREDIENTS

2 pounds sharp white cheddar *(Grafton 1 year works nicely), grated*

8 ounces cream cheese, *softened*

1/2 cup Duke's mayonnaise

4 (4-ounce) jars pimentos, *drained*

1/2 sweet yellow onion, *diced fine*

1 garlic clove, *minced*

1/4 teaspoon cayenne pepper

Salt to taste

Bread of your choice *(Busy Corner uses sourdough.)*

Butter

2 tablespoons Pickled Green Tomato Relish *(You can purchase it at Busy Corner.)*

DIRECTIONS:

Mix the cheese, cream cheese, mayonnaise, pimentos, onion, garlic, cayenne, and salt together until creamy and spreadable. Spread the bread with the pimento cheese. Heat a griddle or skillet. Butter bread and grill on both sides until golden brown. Garnish with Pickled Green Tomato Relish.

Baja Shrimp Tacos

SNAPPER GRABBER'S COASTAL KITCHEN FOOD TRUCK & SEAFOOD MARKET

521 Montgomery Highway, Suite 101
Vestavia Hills, Alabama 35216
Store: 205-824-9799 | SnapperGrabbers.com

ESTABLISHED: Store 2003, Food truck 2013

KNOWN FOR: Fresh Alabama Gulf seafood. Snapper Grabber's in Vestavia is one of the best outlets in the area for seafood, and the truck always features the freshest shrimp, oysters, and grouper from our Gulf waters. In the fall, the truck serves its famous gumbo; arrive early to make sure you get a cup.

DON'T MISS: The Grouper Sandwich and the Oyster Po'boy. They have quite a following of fans who seek out the truck to get their beach-food fix. Check out their daily specials, too. The Crab Cake Sliders have a fine dining flair with a perfect crab-to-breading ratio.

VESTAVIA HILLS AND FOOD TRUCK

BAJA SHRIMP TACOS

Yield: 8 tacos

INGREDIENTS

1/4 cup peanut oil

2 pounds medium Alabama wild-caught Gulf shrimp, *peeled & deveined*

4 tablespoons Baja Seasoning *(See recipe below.)*

8 (6-inch) flour tortillas

2 cups lettuce, finely shredded

1 cup queso fresco, crumbled *(The Mexican white cheese can be found at most grocery stores.)*

Pico de Gallo *(See recipe below or buy your favorite store brand.)*

Lime Crema *(See recipe below.)*

1/4 cup purple cabbage, *finely shredded for garnish*

8 lime wedges

Baja Seasoning:

1 tablespoon paprika

1 1/2 tablespoons oregano

1 tablespoon granulated sugar

1 teaspoon cumin

1 1/2 teaspoons garlic power

1 1/2 teaspoons onion powder

1 1/2 teaspoons kosher salt

1 1/2 teaspoons black pepper

Pico de Gallo:

4 Roma tomatoes, *diced*

2 jalapeño peppers, *seeded and finely diced*

1/4 cup onion, *finely diced*

1/2 small bunch of fresh cilantro, *chopped*

Juice of 1 lime

Sea salt and pepper to taste

Lime Crema:

8 ounces sour cream or Mexican crema

Zest of 1 lime

Juice of 1/2 lime

DIRECTIONS:

For the Baja Seasoning: Mix all dry spices together and set aside.

For the Pico de Gallo: Mix ingredients together and chill.

For the Lime Crema: Mix ingredients together and chill.

For the filling: Heat peanut oil in a large sauté pan on medium-high heat. Toss the shrimp in the heated peanut oil to coat. Sauté for 30 seconds and add 4 tablespoons Baja Seasoning. Stir the shrimp to coat with seasoning and cook for 3-4 minutes until shrimp are thoroughly cooked.

To assemble: Warm or lightly brown the tortillas in a dry skillet or lightly char directly on the open flame of a gas stovetop eye for about 5 seconds per side.

Fill the tortillas with shrimp, lettuce, queso fresco, Pico de Gallo, and Lime Crema. Garnish with purple cabbage and a lime wedge.

Grass-Fed Beef Willis Burger

SHINDIGS CATERING & FOOD TRUCK

3916 Clairmont Avenue
Birmingham, Alabama 35222
Business Line: 205-994-0460
Order Line: 205-704-9131 | ShindigsCateringTrucks.com

ESTABLISHED: 2011. Chef Russell's new brick-and-mortar location, Whistling Table, is set to open in 2017.

KNOWN FOR: Locally sourced fast food. Chef Mac Russell has built a cult following of fans who travel around town to find the Shindigs truck for their mid-day fix. The local ingredients and techniques Mac uses are what you'd find at a fine-dining establishment—this one just happens to be on wheels. The truck is out for breakfast, lunch, and dinner as well as catering and special events. Look on their social media sites for locations and times.

DON'T MISS: Shindigs' steamed Korean-style buns filled with beef short ribs are absolutely one of the best bites in Birmingham. The Willis Burger is also always on the list of the city's top burgers. Get a side of truffle fries to go with your Willis; it's a decadent combo you must try. If you're craving a big salad, they've got that, too.

FOOD TRUCK

GRASS-FED BEEF WILLIS BURGER

Yield: 1 extra deluxe burger

INGREDIENTS

8 ounces local grass fed ground beef, *portioned into 2-4-ounce balls*

4 tablespoons Special Sauce *(See recipe below.)*

2 1/2 tablespoons Fig Mostarda *(See recipe below.)*

2 tablespoons Truffle Yogurt *(See recipe below.)*

2 slices Applewood bacon, *cooked crispy*

1 1/2 ounces bleu cheese

5 tablespoons Garlic Butter *(See recipe below.)*

1/4 cup organic arugula

1 1/2 teaspoons lemon oil

1 1/2 teaspoons salt

1 bun

Special Sauce:

1 cup Worcestershire

1/2 cup balsamic vinegar

1 fresh bay leaf (laurel)

1 Morita chili, *crushed*

4 sprigs fresh thyme

1 tablespoon black peppercorns

1 1/2 teaspoons onion powder

1 1/2 teaspoons garlic powder

Roasted Garlic Butter:

2 heads garlic, with 2 cloves reserved for the Truffle Yogurt

2 sticks unsalted butter

2 cups extra virgin olive oil

Fig Mostarda:

2 large Vidalia onions, *julienned*

2 quarts local figs, *trimmed*

1/2 cup red wine

1/2 cup Acai juice

2 cups balsamic vinegar

1 cup sorghum syrup

1 teaspoon vanilla bean paste *(available at most cooking supply stores)*

3 tablespoons Chinese mustard powder *(available at most Asian markets)*

2 tablespoons fresh thyme

Truffle Yogurt:

1 cup Greek yogurt

1 tablespoon of garlic butter

1/4 teaspoon fresh ground black pepper

1/4 teaspoon fresh lemon juice

1/4 teaspoon truffle salt *(available at kitchen/cook supply stores)*

1/4 teaspoon white truffle oil *(available at kitchen/cook supply stores)*

1 tablespoon Fines-Herbes, chopped *(Typically fresh parsley, tarragon, chives, and chervil are used.)*

GRASS-FED BEEF WILLIS BURGER

(continued)

DIRECTIONS:

For the Special Sauce: Put everything in a pot. Steep for 30 minutes. Strain into a glass jar and set aside.

For the Garlic Butter: Put everything in a pot. Bring to a boil; lower heat to simmer for 30 minutes. Strain into a glass jar and set aside.

For the Fig Mostarda: Trim figs and onions. Add 2 tablespoons of garlic butter to a large pot or saucepan. Cook until caramelized, and then add thyme. Deglaze with the red wine, Acai, and balsamic vinegar. Add sorghum and vanilla, and then let simmer for 30 minutes to reduce. Make a slurry by combining the mustard powder and hot water to make paste. Add after the 30 minutes to thicken the Mostarda. Pour into a food processor. Pulse until slightly chunky but spreadable. Set aside.

For the Truffle Yogurt: Combine ingredients and set aside.

To assemble: Brush the insides of the top and bottom of the bun with the garlic butter. Toast on a griddle or hot cast iron skillet. Smear the bun top with the Fig Mostarda. Smear the bottom bun with the Truffle Yogurt. Season arugula with salt, pepper, and lemon oil and place on top and bottom buns. Season the beef, place the 2-4 ounce balls of beef on the very hot griddle, and press thin with a very hot grill press right away to flatten. Cook until caramelized, about 1-1 1/2 minutes. Flip and immediately baste with Special Sauce. With speedy intentions, top one patty with bleu cheese and the slice of bacon. Rapidly repeat with the other patty. Stack the patties together and place on the bottom bun. Finally, place other bun on top and proceed to eat.

Main Courses

Saw's Soul Kitchen
▶▶ BBQ Pork n'Greens 154

Ocean
▶▶ Grilled Whole Gulf Snapper 158

Gianmarco's Restaurant
▶▶ Penne alla Vodka 160

Miss Dots
▶▶ Flat-Top Roasted Chicken 162

Jim 'N Nick's Bar-B-Q
▶▶ Bar-B-Q Rub 164

Taj India
▶▶ Chicken Tikka Masala 166

The Bright Star
▶▶ Tenderloin of Beef Greek Style 168

Little Savannah Restaurant and Bar
▶▶ Crab Cakes 170

The Gardens Café
▶▶ Tomato Pie 172

The Fish Market Southside
▶▶ George's Stuffed Rainbow Trout 174

Blackwell's Pub & Eatery
▶▶ Shepherd's Pie 176

Vino
▶▶ Eggplant Chicken Capellini 178

Satterfield's Restaurant
▶▶ Coddled Egg Over Creamy Gulf Shrimp 180

Silvertron Café
▶▶ Pork Shank Silvertron 182

Ted's Restaurant
▶▶ Souvlakia 184

Giuseppe's Café
▶▶ Chicken and Prosciutto Pasta 186

dg
▶▶ Pork Picatta dg 188

Nabeel's Café & Market
▶▶ Moussaka 190

SAW'S SOUL KITCHEN

215 41st Street South
Birmingham, AL 35222
205-591-1409 | SawsBBQ.com

ESTABLISHED: 2012

KNOWN FOR: Award-winning barbecue and killer greens. A key player in Avondale's revitalization, Saw's has become a landmark Southern barbecue haven. Located next door to Avondale Brewery, the local brew and killer barbecue combo first brought in the locals, then the press, and the crowds soon followed. If you don't want barbecue, you'll find a chalkboard menu with lots of options including chicken, burgers, smoked sausage, and shrimp 'n grits.

DON'T MISS: This one! Pork n'Greens with the fried onions on top is the most popular dish on the menu, but if you want to try something else, go for the Sweet Tea Fried Chicken or the Smoked Wings. The Smoked Chicken with White BBQ Sauce is also a sure thing. Ask about dessert; hopefully, banana pudding will be on the menu when you visit.

SAW'S BBQ PORK N'GREENS

Yield: Serves 4-5, with pork left over for another use

INGREDIENTS

Pulled Pork:

1 small (8-10 pound) bone-in pork butt *(shoulder)*

1/2 cup yellow mustard

1 cup Saw's Rub

Hickory wood for smoker

Turnip Greens:

4 ounces bacon, *cut into 1/4-inch pieces*

1 yellow onion, *julienned*

2 1/2 pounds turnip greens, *chopped and rinsed*

1 1/2 quarts water

1 tablespoon Lawry's Seasoned Salt

1 cup Saw's Sauce

1 teaspoon fresh ground black pepper

Cheese Grits:

3 1/2 cups water

1 teaspoon kosher salt

1 cup McEwen and Sons™ Stone Ground Grits

1 cup whole milk

2 tablespoons unsalted butter

2 cups cheddar cheese, *shredded*

Fried Onions:

1 yellow onion, *sliced as thinly as possible, preferably on slicer or Japanese mandolin*

1 small can evaporated milk

1 small box Zataran's® seasoned cornmeal

Oil for frying

Saw's BBQ Pork N'Greens

SAW'S BBQ PORK N'GREENS

(continued)

DIRECTIONS:

For the pulled pork: Coat pork butt with thin layer of yellow mustard on all sides. Pour rub into large bowl and dip butt on all sides, making sure there is a uniform layer of seasoning on all sides.

Smoke with hickory wood at 275° Fahrenheit, fat side up, for 6-8 hours until bone starts to protrude from the butt, fat cap has softened, and desired color has been achieved. Remove from smoker, wrap with heavy duty aluminum foil, and return to heat. Cook another 4-6 hours until butt is soft to the touch and bone comes out with no resistance.

To serve pork, unwrap from foil, using tongs remove the bone. Separate the meat from the remaining pieces of fat inside the butt.

For the greens: In large pot, cook bacon until crispy; add onions and sweat until soft. Add greens, along with water, Lawry's, sauce, and pepper. Bring to a boil, lower to simmer, and cook until greens are tender, approximately 1 1/2 hours. Adjust seasoning as needed with Saw's sauce and seasoned salt.

For the grits: Bring water and salt to a boil, and then whisk in grits until well combined with no lumps. Stir frequently, bring to a boil, reduce heat to a simmer, and cook until the grits are tender and most of the liquid is absorbed.

In small saucepan, heat milk until just below boiling, and add it slowly to grits and then stir to combine. Continue to cook until liquid is absorbed into grits. Add butter and cheese; stir well and cook until melted and combined. Adjust consistency as desired with extra milk or water, and add salt as needed.

For the onions: In medium bowl, soak onions in evaporated milk for at least 1 minute.

Pour cornmeal in separate bowl, remove onions from milk mixture, allow excess to drip off, and dredge them into cornmeal. Shake well to remove all excess breading.

Deep fry at 350° for approximately 30-45 seconds or until crispy.

For assembly: Carefully ladle 8 ounces of the cheese grits onto a large plate and spread to form a uniform layer. Top with 6 ounces of well-drained turnip greens, 6 ounces of pulled pork, and 2 ounces of Saw's Sauce. Top with fried onions.

Grilled Whole Gulf Snapper

OCEAN

1218 20th Street South
Birmingham, Alabama 35205
205-933-0999 | OceanBirmingham.com

ESTABLISHED: 2002

KNOWN FOR: Fresh Gulf seafood, superbly prepared by Chef George Reis, one of the region's premier seafood chefs and winner of the Alabama Seafood Cook-off in 2015. Start at the bar for a custom cocktail and order a dozen oysters from the raw bar. Share the whole fish (the selection changes daily) or indulge in the whole Maine lobster. Save room for the elaborate selection of house-made desserts like the caramel lava cake or seasonal ice cream.

DON'T MISS: The Seafood Tower filled with oysters, clams, lobster, and shrimp. Invite a few friends for happy hour after work, order a bottle of bubbly, and share; it is the perfect way to end a long work day. The Oysters Rockefeller are broiled until bubbly and topped with spinach, bacon, and Manchego cheese. Try the Thai Green Curry Bouillabaisse with lobster tail, Gulf shrimp, mussels, red grouper, clams, and pineapple jasmine rice; it hits all the right notes—sweet, spicy, tangy, and citrus.

SOUTHSIDE

GRILLED WHOLE GULF SNAPPER

Yield: Serves 1-2, depending on size of fish

INGREDIENTS

1 whole (1-2 pound) red snapper

4 tablespoons extra-virgin olive oil, *divided*

2 tablespoons kosher salt

1 teaspoon cracked black pepper

1 tablespoon fresh oregano, *chopped*

2 cloves garlic, *chopped*

Baker's Joy Baking Spray

2 lemons, *cut in half*

DIRECTIONS:

Preheat the grill to medium-high heat. If you're using charcoal, allow the coals to burn halfway down.

Rub entire outside of fish with 1 tablespoon olive oil. Next, generously season outside of fish with salt, pepper, oregano, and garlic. Spray completely with Baker's Joy. Place fish on grill to cook. Cook the fish 10 minutes per inch of the thickness of the fish. (For example, a fish 2 inches thick should cook about 20 minutes or 10 minutes per side of the fish.) Turn after about 10 minutes and baste with olive oil. Squeeze the juice of the lemons over fish. Baste frequently with olive oil for the next 10 minutes.

Remove carefully from grill. Place on large serving platter. If you need to add a bit more flare, accompany the fish with fresh sautéed vegetables. Don't be afraid to squeeze more lemon on it.

Penne Alla Vodka

GIANMARCO'S RESTAURANT

721 Broadway Street
Birmingham, Alabama 35209
205-871-9622 | GiammarcosBhm.com

ESTABLISHED: 2003

KNOWN FOR: Charming, authentic, upscale Italian restaurant with family roots in New York City. Casual yet sophisticated and nestled into the toney Edgewood neighborhood, Gianmarco's menu offers superb Italian comfort food, made-from-scratch pasta, exceptional steaks, and daily specials from Chef Michael Brady. Owners Gianni and Marco Respinto grew up in their father Gio's New York restaurant, and Gianmarco's reflects their family heritage. They have a sweet little wine shop and bar behind the restaurant; quaint and intimate, it is a great date night spot or place to catch-up with girlfriends.

DON'T MISS: The ribeye. The meatballs get rave reviews and many requests for the recipe, but it is the Penne Alla Vodka that has been the most requested recipe since the doors opened.

HOMEWOOD

GIANMARCO'S PENNE ALLA VODKA

Yield: Serves 2-4, depending on portion size

INGREDIENTS

1/4 cup frozen or fresh English peas

1 cup high quality penne pasta

1/2 cup diced pancetta *(GianMarco's is made in-house; you can buy pancetta at most grocery stores.)*

1/2 cup onion, *chopped*

1/2 cup Portobello and Cremini mushrooms, *sliced*

2 tablespoons butter, *divided*

Chicken, sausage, or shrimp if desired

2 tablespoons vodka

1/2 cup marinara *(Homemade is the best option.)*

2 teaspoons heavy cream

Salt and pepper to taste

Freshly grated Parmesan cheese

4 large leaves of fresh basil, *chiffonade, for garnish*

DIRECTIONS:

Blanch the English peas in boiling water until tender. Immediately submerge in an ice bath to preserve their color. Strain and set aside.

Cook the pasta according to package instructions. Strain and set aside.

Sauté pancetta until fat is slightly rendered. Add onions, mushrooms, and one pat of butter. (If desired, add chicken or another protein of your choice.) Sauté until onion is translucent and protein is slightly brown. Remove the pan from the heat and deglaze with the vodka. Return to the heat and add marinara. Continue to cook until the protein is thoroughly cooked.

Add heavy cream, peas, and cooked penne pasta. Season with salt and pepper to taste. As soon as pasta is evenly coated, place in a large serving bowl. Garnish with grated Parmesan cheese and fresh basil.

Flat-Top Roasted Chicken

MISS DOTS

49 Church Street
Mountain Brook, Alabama 35213
205-739-2232 | LoveMissDots.com

ESTABLISHED: 2015

KNOWN FOR: Their famous fried chicken and Darn Good Pecan Pie. If you love chicken — fried, roasted, or hot — put Miss Dots at the top of your must-try list. The restaurant is named for Leola "Miss Dot" Rogers, a longtime friend of founder John Cassimus. After years of requests from friends and family, the two opened their first location in Crestline and a second location soon afterward in Tuscaloosa.

DON'T MISS: Their homemade squash casserole. It is heaven in a bowl. Their newest must-try dish is the Dot's Dip with fire-roasted peppers, cheese, and their famous chicken, served with Fritos Scoops®.

CRESTLINE VILLAGE

FLAT-TOP ROASTED CHICKEN

Yield: 8 pieces

INGREDIENTS

1 whole chicken

2 teaspoons salt

2 teaspoons pepper

2 teaspoons garlic powder

2 teaspoons fresh thyme, *minced*

2 teaspoons fresh oregano, *minced*

2 teaspoons fresh rosemary, *minced*

DIRECTIONS:

Note: Requires 12 hours in the refrigerator before baking

Clean the chicken. Spatchcock the chicken by removing the backbone with kitchen shears or a sharp knife. You can ask the butcher or someone at the meat counter to do this for you, but it really is easy to do.

Mix the salt, pepper, garlic, thyme, oregano, and rosemary together and sprinkle over both sides of the chicken.

Line a baking sheet with aluminum foil. Flatten the chicken on the baking sheet, back side down. Let sit in the refrigerator, uncovered, for 12 hours. This will dry out the skin, keeping it crispy and helping to seal in those essential juices.

Preheat oven to 350° Fahrenheit. Bake for 90 minutes or until internal temperature has reached 165°. Remove from oven and allow to rest for 10-12 minutes before slicing.

Jim 'N Nick's Bar-B-Q Rub

JIM 'N NICK'S BAR-B-Q

Nick Pihakis,
James Beard Award Semi-Finalist

Alabaster | Birmingham Airport | Five Points South | Greystone
Gardendale | Homewood | Riverchase | Trussville
JimnNicks.com

ESTABLISHED: In 1985, Nick Pihakis and his dad, Jim, opened the first Jim 'N Nick's restaurant on Clairmont Avenue in Birmingham. Today, Jim 'N Nick's boasts 34-plus restaurants in 7 states and is regarded as a Southern barbecue tradition. The chain is ever-evolving by incorporating sustainable products into the menu and breeding its own heritage pork.

KNOWN FOR: Barbecue pork, ribs, and sides. The restaurant's most popular item may just be their light and airy cheese biscuits. After a million requests for the recipe, they now sell the mix in their restaurants and grocery stores around the country. While not exactly the top secret rub used in their restaurants, the rub recipe in this book is very close to the original and often used by the Jim 'N Nick's team for barbecue and other food events across the country.

DON'T MISS: The Baby Back Ribs or the Loaded Bar-B-Q Baker, which is a giant baked potato stuffed with pulled pork and classic toppings. The chicken fingers, which are some of the best ones around, are not just for kids.

LOCAL CHAIN

JIM 'N NICK'S BAR-B-Q RUB

Yield: 2 cups

INGREDIENTS

1 cup kosher salt
1/2 cup granulated sugar
1/2 cup brown sugar
1/2 cup paprika
2 tablespoons ground black pepper
1 teaspoon cayenne pepper

DIRECTIONS:

Combine all ingredients in a mixing bowl and whisk together to evenly blend all ingredients. The rub will store well for several months, covered and away from heat, but is best used quickly while the spices are fresh.

Note: This is a great base to use alone on any meat, especially pork, but it is also a good base to use as a foundation. Add spices to this base recipe to create a unique rub tweaked with your favorite flavors. Make it in large batches to give as a gift for the holidays to the pit master or grill queen in your circle.

TAJ INDIA

2226 Highland Avenue South
Birmingham, Alabama 35205
205-939-3805 | TajIndia.net

ESTABLISHED: 1986

KNOWN FOR: Authentic Indian favorites like Chicken Tikka Masala, Dal, Pakoras, Curry, Naan bread, and Lamb Roganjosh. You'll even find exotic specialties like Goat Curry and Lamb Vindaloo. As a Southside institution and Birmingham's oldest Indian restaurant, it has drawn area families to line up for the legendary buffet for generations. Located in the same strip with the Western on Highland Avenue, Taj India is a great spot for date night or lunch with the office crew.

DON'T MISS: Sag Paneer (cheese and spinach casserole) is everyone's favorite. Anything from the tandoori oven is a sure bet. If you like lentils, you'll love the Dal, and if they have the special Dal Soup, order it. Made with yellow lentils, it is slightly spicy and very warm and comforting. Another excellent choice is the Chicken Korma—chicken cooked in a spiced coconut cream sauce with nuts, raisins, and saffron.

Taj India Chicken Tikka Masala

TAJ INDIA
CHICKEN TIKKA MASALA

INGREDIENTS

Chicken Tikka:

3 tablespoons ginger paste

3 tablespoons garlic paste

Salt to taste

3 teaspoons lemon juice

2 tablespoons vegetable oil

1 teaspoon chili powder

1 teaspoon garam masala *(Find it in the spice aisle or make your own.)*

1/2 teaspoon ground cumin

1 teaspoon ground coriander

1 cup yogurt, *beaten well*

1 3/4 pounds boneless chicken, *cut into cubes (about 3 1/2 cups)*

Masala:

3 tablespoons vegetable oil

3 teaspoons ginger paste

3-4 teaspoons garlic paste

2 teaspoons Kashmiri chili powder

1/4 teaspoon ground turmeric

2 teaspoons ground coriander powder

2 teaspoons garam masala

3 tablespoons tomato puree

Salt to taste

1 cup coconut cream

Coriander leaves, *chopped, for garnish (Americans call this cilantro.)*

DIRECTIONS:

For the Chicken Tikka: In a large bowl or zip-top bag, combine all the Chicken Tikka ingredients except the chicken, and whisk or shake to combine. Add the chicken and marinate for 1 hour.

Preheat the oven to 300° Fahrenheit.

Remove the chicken from the marinade to a baking sheet and bake until the chicken is completely done, about 40 minutes. You can also grill the chicken if you prefer.

For the Masala: Heat oil in a heavy pan. Add ginger and garlic pastes and let them fry until the oil separates. Add the chili, turmeric, coriander, and garam masala, and then add tomato puree. Add salt to taste and then add a little warm water.

Finally add the cooked chicken pieces, and let the sauce come to a boil. Let it cook for another 3-4 minutes or until the sauce thickens. Add the coconut cream and cook for another 2 minutes. Remove the pan from the heat and add the chopped coriander (cilantro) leaves for garnish.

The Bright Star Tenderloin of Beef Greek Style

THE BRIGHT STAR

James Beard Award Winner

304 19th Street North
Bessemer, Alabama 35020
205-424-9444 | TheBrightStar.com

ESTABLISHED: 1907

KNOWN FOR: The Broiled Seafood Platter, Tenderloin of Beef Greek Style, Snapper Almondine, mile-high pies, and Greek specialties. This Alabama institution first opened in 1907 and quickly outgrew 3 locations before moving to its current location in 1914. It has far too many accolades and awards to mention, but foremost among them, the restaurant received the prestigious American Classics Award from the James Beard Foundation in 2010.

DON'T MISS: The fresh Gulf seafood, delivered daily from the coast. The Gulf Snapper Throats is one of the most popular menu items. Try to attend the restaurant's annual New Orleans event or one of their visiting chef dinners. Be certain to order the coconut pie, and check out the hand-painted murals on the walls.

BESSEMER

THE BRIGHT STAR TENDERLOIN of BEEF GREEK STYLE

Yield: Serves 4

INGREDIENTS

4 (10-ounce) beef tenderloin steaks, *butterflied*

2 cups olive oil

1/2 cup lemon juice, *divided*

2 tablespoons garlic, *minced, divided*

2 teaspoons dried oregano, *divided*

Salt and pepper to taste

6 ounces (1 1/2 sticks) butter

DIRECTIONS:

Clean the steaks, trimming away any silver skin, fat, or connective tissue. Butterfly each filet and set aside.

Add the olive oil, 6 tablespoons lemon juice, 11/2 tablespoons garlic, and 1 teaspoon oregano, along with the salt and pepper to taste, to a plastic zip-top bag or a Pyrex dish large enough to fit all of the steaks. Add the steaks and marinate in the refrigerator for 2-3 hours, turning occasionally. Remove from the refrigerator at least 45 minutes prior to cooking.

Place a rack closest to the broiler. Preheat the broiler. Place a large broiler pan on the rack to heat.

In a saucepan, melt the butter and add the remaining lemon juice, garlic, and oregano. Mix thoroughly and set aside.

Remove the steaks from the marinade. Using tongs and an oven mitt, carefully place the steaks on the hot pan and broil to the desired degree of doneness, turning only once. You will likely cook the steaks for about 4 minutes per side, depending on the degree of doneness you prefer. Remove the steaks from the oven and transfer to serving plate. Tent with foil and allow to rest for 2 minutes. Remove the foil, add 3 tablespoons of the butter sauce to each steak, and serve.

Note: Use a meat thermometer for the best results: 140° Fahrenheit = medium rare, 155° Fahrenheit = medium. Keep in mind the meat will continue to cook and increase approximately 5 additional degrees once you remove it from the oven.

Little Savannah's Crab Cakes

LITTLE SAVANNAH RESTAURANT AND BAR

3811 Clairmont Avenue
Birmingham, Alabama 35222
205-591-1119 | LittleSavannah.com

ESTABLISHED: 2003

KNOWN FOR: Farm-to-table dinners. Chef Clifton Holt had been hosting these with his farmers long before they became trendy. The menu is full of seasonal produce, locally sourced meat, and fresh Gulf seafood. This restaurant's intimate atmosphere makes it perfect for date night or a special occasion.

DON'T MISS: Little Savannah's Shrimp and Grits, which has been on the menu from the beginning and is on the Alabama Tourism Department's list of 100 Dishes to Eat in Alabama Before You Die. The recipe is featured in the *Birmingham's Best Bites* cookbook. When you visit, save room for one of the restaurant's daily indulgences like the Blueberry and Peach Sopapillas with mascarpone and local honey.

FOREST PARK

LITTLE SAVANNAH'S CRAB CAKE

Yield: 4 as an appetizer or entrée portion, but cakes can be made smaller for hors d'oeuvres

INGREDIENTS

2 tablespoons unsalted butter

3 tablespoons shallots, *minced*

3 tablespoons red bell pepper, *minced*

3 tablespoons Poblano pepper, *minced*

1 large egg

1/2 teaspoon Dijon mustard

Dash Tabasco

Zest of 1 lemon

1 pound fresh lump crab meat, *picked for shell fragments*

3 tablespoons Panko bread crumbs

2 tablespoons parsley, *minced*

Salt and pepper to taste

DIRECTIONS:

Preheat oven on broil.

In a skillet or saucepan, lightly sauté shallots and peppers in butter for 1 minute. Remove from heat and cool completely.

Beat together the egg, mustard, Tabasco, and lemon zest.

Gently mix the crabmeat with all other ingredients until just combined. Do not overmix or you will break down the crab. Carefully form the mixture into patties. Use 1 ounce for hors d'oeuvres; use 4 ounces for an appetizer portion.

Place the patties on a baking sheet and broil for approximately 10 minutes until light golden brown.

Serve with Rémoulade, cocktail, or mustard sauce.

Notes

THE GARDEN'S CAFÉ BY KATHY G

At Birmingham Botanical Gardens

2612 Lane Park Road
Mountain Brook, Alabama 35223
205-871-1000 | KathyG.com/Venues/Gardens-Cafe

ESTABLISHED: 2011

KNOWN FOR: The setting paired with catering guru Kathy Mezrano of Kathy G & Company's creative cuisine. It's the ideal "ladies who lunch" spot and perfect for a wedding shower or bridesmaid luncheon, too. You can even get Kathy's famous honey mustard chicken salad or anything else on the menu to-go to enjoy anywhere inside the gardens. The central location and the magnificent setting make the café a great choice for a wedding or corporate event.

DON'T MISS: The Quiche of the Day. Second only to the Chicken Salad Plate, it features a flaky crust and seasonal flavors. Sit inside on a chilly fall day and watch the leaves turn in the garden over a bowl of homemade soup or a hearty salad. Try the Pear Salad: mixed greens with red wine poached pears, dried cranberries, toasted walnuts, and goat cheese with a light and tangy raspberry vinaigrette. You can get many of Kathy's recipes and entertaining tips in her book, *Food, Fun & Fabulous*.

Kathy G's Tomato Pie

MOUNTAIN BROOK VILLAGE

KATHY G'S TOMATO PIE

Yield: 6-8 slices, depending on portion size

INGREDIENTS

1 (9-inch) pie crust, *baked*

4 Roma tomatoes, *sliced*

1/2 cup balsamic vinegar

3 tablespoons fresh basil, *chopped*

1 yellow onion, *sliced*

2 cloves garlic, *minced*

2 tablespoons olive oil

3/4 cup real mayonnaise

1/2 cup Parmesan cheese, *grated*

1 cup crumbled Feta cheese

Salt and pepper to taste

DIRECTIONS:

Preheat oven to 350° Fahrenheit.

Bake the pie crust according to package directions. Set aside.

Pour the vinegar over the tomatoes and let them marinate for about 10 minutes, and then drain and season with salt and pepper. Mix the tomatoes with the basil.

In a skillet or saucepan, sauté the onions and garlic together in the olive oil over medium heat until they are soft and begin to turn golden brown, about 10 minutes. If they begin to stick to the pan, you can add about 1 tablespoon water.

In a separate bowl, combine mayonnaise and both cheeses. Layer the tomato and basil mixture in the bottom of the baked pie shell. Spread sautéed onions on top of the tomatoes. Spread the mayonnaise and cheese mixture over the top.

Bake for about 35 minutes or until lightly browned on the top.

Notes

George's Stuffed Rainbow Trout

THE FISH MARKET SOUTHSIDE

612 22nd Street South
Birmingham, Alabama 35233
205-322-3330 | TheFishMarket.net

ESTABLISHED: 1982

KNOWN FOR: Fresh fish, whole lobster, and Greek hospitality. Chef/Owner George Sarris is a larger-than-life local celebrity. You may frequently see him cooking on morning news programs, and you always see him walking through the restaurant, welcoming his guests. The Grilled Seafood Platter and the Athenian Style Snapper are two of George's signature dishes, but it is his stuffed fish recipe that was the most requested.

DON'T MISS: Seafood gumbo or the Cioppino. George says he has customers who come in for both dishes even when the weather is hot outside. George's Shrimp Saganaki with fresh Gulf shrimp is another dish diners don't want to miss. The Cioppino and Saginaki recipes are featured in *Birmingham's Best Bites*.

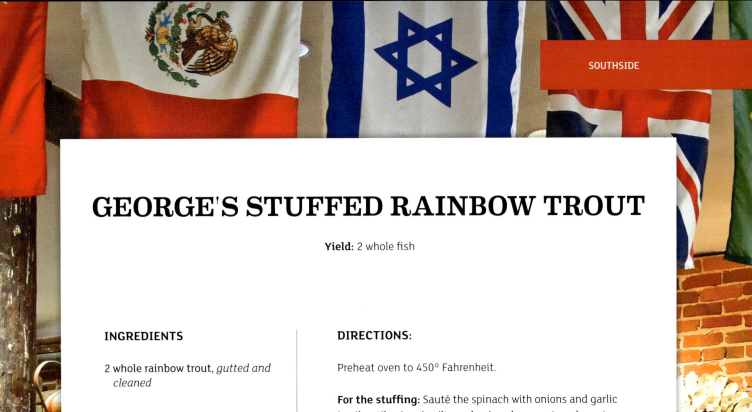

SOUTHSIDE

GEORGE'S STUFFED RAINBOW TROUT

Yield: 2 whole fish

INGREDIENTS

2 whole rainbow trout, *gutted and cleaned*

Stuffing:

3 cups fresh spinach leaves, *stems removed*

1/4 cup red onion, *diced*

1/4 cup white onion, *diced*

1 clove garlic, *minced*

1/2 cup roasted red pepper, *chopped*

1 cup popcorn shrimp, *boiled and chopped*

1/4 cup artichoke hearts, *chopped*

1 tablespoon Greek seasoning

Coarse salt and cracked black pepper to taste

3/4 cup Panko bread crumbs

3 tablespoons George's extra-virgin olive oil

DIRECTIONS:

Preheat oven to 450° Fahrenheit.

For the stuffing: Sauté the spinach with onions and garlic in oil until spinach wilts and onions become translucent. Remove from the heat and fold in remaining ingredients.

Stuff each fish with the mixture and bake in the preheated oven for 5-7 minutes or until cooked through. Cooking time will be determined by how large the fish is and how much stuffing you add to each one.

To serve: Drizzle with a bit more extra virgin olive oil and a squeeze of fresh lemon juice on the fish.

Blackwell's Shepherd's Pie

BLACKWELL'S PUB & EATERY

Market Square Shopping Center
3151 Green Valley Road
Birmingham, Alabama 35243
205-967-3798 | BlackwellsPub.com

ESTABLISHED: 2009

KNOWN FOR: British pub food meets Alabama bar and comfort food favorites. Your mama's meatloaf goes British with Blackwell's signature sauce. This is one of the few places in Birmingham where you'll find Shepherd's Pie on the menu; it's a customer favorite made from scratch and topped with creamy mashed potatoes and melted cheddar.

DON'T MISS: The award-winning PB&J Burger, made with blackberry jam and smooth peanut butter. Fans swear it is the best burger anywhere. Check out the vast selection of imported beers, including unique sweet brews like Wells Sticky Toffee Pudding or Banana Bread brews from Bedford, England.

CAHABA HEIGHTS

BLACKWELL'S SHEPHERD'S PIE

Yield: Serves 2-4 depending on portion size

INGREDIENTS

Mashed potatoes:

3 pounds baking potatoes, *peeled and cubed*

4 tablespoons unsalted butter

1/2 cup sour cream

Salt and pepper to taste

Filling:

2 tablespoons olive oil

1 tablespoon butter

1 cup yellow onion, *diced*

1 cup carrots, *diced small*

1 teaspoon garlic, *minced*

2 pounds 80/20 ground sirloin

1 (15-ounce) can sweet peas, *drained*

Gravy:

1/3 cup reserved beef drippings

1/3 cup all-purpose flour

3 cups beef broth

1/4 teaspoon salt

1/8 teaspoon pepper

Topping:

1/2 cup cheddar cheese, *shredded*

DIRECTIONS:

Preheat oven to 350° Fahrenheit.

For the potatoes: Add cubed potatoes to a large pot and cover with cool water. Bring to a boil over high heat. Cook until fork tender. Drain. Add butter, sour cream, and salt and pepper to taste. Mash using a hand mixer or masher to the consistency you desire. Set aside.

For the filling: In a large cast iron skillet over medium heat, heat olive oil and butter. When butter melts, add the diced onions and carrots, and sauté for 2 minutes or until tender. Add the garlic and cook 1 minute more. Add beef and sauté until browned. Drain the beef, reserving the drippings for the gravy. Add the peas to the beef and set aside.

For the gravy: Add 1/3 cup drippings back to the skillet. Once hot, whisk the flour into drippings. Cook, stirring constantly, over medium heat for 2-3 minutes or until smooth and light brown. Add broth, 1 cup at a time, whisking constantly until mixture boils and thickens, about 5-7 minutes. Stir in salt and pepper. Remove from heat. Pour into a heatproof container, measuring out 1 cup of gravy. Set aside. (Note: Use the leftover gravy to serve on the side or for another use.)

To assemble: Return filling mixture to the skillet. Stir in the reserved cup of gravy. Season with salt and pepper. Reduce heat to low and simmer for 5 minutes. Remove from heat. Cover the filling with mashed potatoes; top with shredded cheese. Place in the oven and cook uncovered for 5 minutes or until cheese is golden brown and melted.

Eggplant Chicken Cappellini

VINO

1930 Cahaba Road
Mountain Brook, Alabama 35223
205-870-8404 | VinoBirmingham.com

ESTABLISHED: 2012

KNOWN FOR: One of the best patios in town, voted by readers in the annual *Birmingham Magazine* "Best of Birmingham" awards. The feel is modern and sleek; the glass walls give the ambiance of dining in a garden. Al Raibee has created a beautiful setting for his cuisine fashioned from local ingredients like fresh seafood, lamb, pasta, and locally grown vegetables.

DON'T MISS: Guests rave about the Rosemary Lamb Shanks and the scallops; the Sesame Crusted Yellowfin Tuna with Soy Basmati Rice is another favorite. Guests return time and again for this Capellini. The recipe is one the chef converted for the home cook.

ENGLISH VILLAGE

EGGPLANT CHICKEN CAPELLINI

Yield: Serves 6-8

INGREDIENTS

Blackening spice, *if desired*

2 large eggplant, *peeled, sliced lengthwise into 1/4-inch slices*

2 cups milk

2 eggs, beaten

2 cups Italian bread crumbs

1/4 cup olive oil plus an additional 2-3 tablespoons

1 cup chopped yellow onion

1 cup chopped celery

1/2 teaspoon ground turmeric

2 whole garlic cloves, *diced*

1 1/2 pound boneless skinless chicken breasts

4 cups tomato basil sauce *(store-bought or homemade)*

1 1/2 - 2 cups chicken stock

1/2 cup medium bodied red wine

2 cups Crimini mushrooms, *sliced*

6-8 ounces shredded Mozzarella

1/2 cups grated Grana Padano

1/2 pound angel hair pasta *(Capellini), cooked al dente in salted water*

DIRECTIONS:

Note: Allow 1 hour extra time for the eggplant preparation. Sprinkle the chicken with blackening spice and set aside.

Slice the eggplant; lightly salt and lay out the slices on paper towels to let the eggplant "breathe" for an hour.

Combine the eggs and milk. Beat thoroughly. Pour into a casserole dish.

Dip each slice of eggplant in the egg mixture then press into the Italian bread crumbs. Shake off the excess.

Add enough olive oil to coat the bottom of a frying pan. Heat the oil over medium-high heat. Add the eggplant and lightly fry each slide until browned and eggplant is tender. Remove to drain on paper towels and set aside.

Add a bit more oil to the pan and heat it over medium-high heat. Sauté the chopped onions, celery, and turmeric until onions are transparent and celery is tender. Add the chopped garlic and sauté another 2-3 minutes.

Add the chicken to the onion and celery mix and lightly brown on each side.

Heat the tomato basil sauce in a small saucepan.

Add chicken stock, red wine, and Crimini mushrooms. Cover and let simmer until chicken is cooked throughout, approximately 10-15 minutes.

Remove the chicken breasts, dice very small, and then return to the onion/celery/mushroom mix.

Place 1/2 cup of chicken mixture and approximately 1 ounce shredded mozzarella onto each cooked eggplant slice. Roll up lengthwise and place the eggplant into a shallow baking pan, seam-side down. Repeat for all eggplant slices. Keep warm in the oven while you cook the pasta.

Place desired amount of cooked pasta on each plate, top with stuffed eggplant and tomato basil sauce, and sprinkle with freshly grated Grana Padano.

Satterfield's Coddled Egg Over Creamy Gulf Shrimp

SATTERFIELD'S RESTAURANT

3161 Cahaba Heights Road
Birmingham, Alabama 35243
205-969-9690 | SatterfieldsRestaurant.com

ESTABLISHED: 2005

KNOWN FOR: Duroc Pork Chop and Chef-Owner Becky Satterfield's desserts. It is a friendly neighborhood place with all of the qualities and nuances of a fine dining establishment. The menu is contemporary Southern with an emphasis on seasonal produce, locally sourced meats, and fresh Gulf seafood. The bar program is impressive with a cocktail list that makes you feel like you're visiting a swanky bar in Manhattan. Try a classic cocktail like the Old Fashioned and The Bee's Knees; they are as good as you'll find anywhere.

DON'T MISS: Live music Wednesdays in the bar. Try The Italian 75, made with Satterfield's house-made Limoncello and a splash of Prosecco. Order a bite to eat and hang out, and maybe Becky Satterfield will even stop by to chat. Make sure to get an order of Becky's famous corn muffins. They are so legendary that customers order them to-go for holiday parties and special occasions, and the recipe was featured in *Birmingham's Best Bites*.

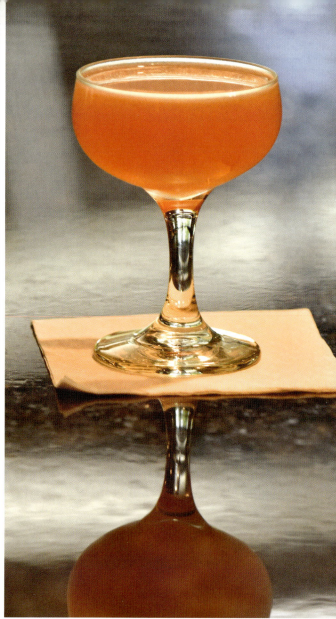

CAHABA HEIGHTS

SATTERFIELD'S CODDLED EGG OVER CREAMY GULF SHRIMP

Yield: Serves 4

INGREDIENTS

1/4 pound andouille sausage, *cubed*

2 tablespoons canola oil

1 small yellow onion, *small diced*

2 ribs celery, *small diced*

1 small green or red bell pepper, *small diced*

1/4 pound fresh watercress, or another bitter green such as frisée or escarole

2 cups heavy cream

Kosher salt and freshly ground black pepper to taste

3-6 dashes Tabasco sauce *(Add more if you like it spicy.)*

1/4 cup Worcestershire sauce

1/4 pound fresh 21/25 count Gulf shrimp, *heads off, peeled, and deveined*

2 teaspoons white vinegar

4 large farm eggs

6 ounces Parmigiano Reggiano, *grated*

DIRECTIONS:

Place the andouille and the canola oil in a medium nonstick pan over medium heat. Once some of the fat is rendered from sausage, add the onion, celery, and bell pepper to the pan and sauté for 3 minutes or until translucent and softened. Add the watercress and heavy cream. Increase the heat to medium-high, bringing the creamy mixture to a boil. Season the mixture with a pinch each of salt and pepper, and add the Tabasco and Worcestershire to taste.

Continue to cook, reducing the cream until it is thick, about 4-5 minutes. During the last 2 minutes of cooking, add the shrimp to the mixture and continue to cook until the shrimp turn pink and curl. Set aside and keep warm. (Note: If the cream is a little runny, remove the shrimp to keep them from overcooking and reduce the sauce further. You want a thick mixture.)

To poach the eggs: Heat about 1 1/2 inches of water in a 12-inch nonstick skillet. Add 1 teaspoon kosher salt and 2 teaspoons white vinegar to the water and bring to a simmer over medium heat. Meanwhile, crack each egg into a small ramekin or custard cup, removing any pieces of shell. Do not stir the water. Drop each egg from the ramekin into the simmering water. Set a timer for 4 minutes. Do not poke, stir, or jostle the egg in any way. Lift each egg out of the water using a slotted spoon, and gently place on a plate. Set aside.

To finish: Preheat oven to 400° Fahrenheit.

Stir the creamy shrimp mixture to incorporate all ingredients. Fill four ramekins with the creamy shrimp mixture, leaving about 1/2 inch at the top. Add a poached egg to each ramekin and top each with grated Parmigiano Reggiano. Set ramekins onto a baking sheet and place in the oven. Set a timer for 4 minutes, checking often. Not all ovens are created equally, so you may have to adjust oven temperature or cooking times. When the cheese is bubbling and starting to brown, it's perfect; remove the baking sheet with the ramekins from the oven. Serve immediately.

SILVERTRON CAFÉ

3813 Clairmont Avenue
Birmingham, Alabama 35222
205-591-3707 | SilvertronCafe.us

ESTABLISHED: Original 1986, Current 2007

KNOWN FOR: Homemade Italian favorites and Southern comfort food classics. Chef and owner Marco Morosini creates a Pasta of the Day special daily and offers bargain pasta specials on Pasta Night each Monday. Other Italian favorites are Chicken Parmigiana and a peppery Fettuccine All'Alfredo. The Birminghammer cocktail combines Buffalo Rock Ginger Ale bottled right here in the Magic City along with local Redmont Gin and ginger syrup. The result is a spicy, effervescent cocktail reminiscent of a Moscow Mule.

DON'T MISS: Sunday brunch. Egg, Steak, Florentine, or Mushroom Benedicts are extremely popular. For dessert, try the White Chocolate Bread Pudding served with whipped cream and raspberry coulis or the Forest Park Pie, a pecan pie topped with chocolate chips, vanilla ice cream, and whipped cream.

Pork Shank Silvertron

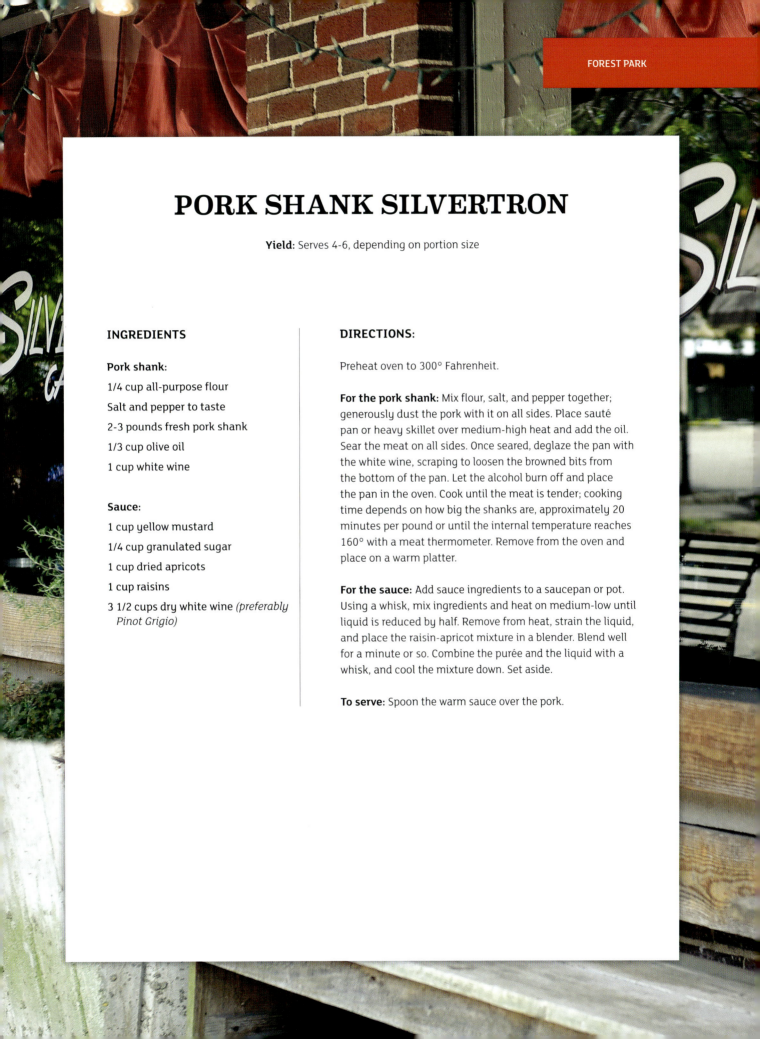

FOREST PARK

PORK SHANK SILVERTRON

Yield: Serves 4-6, depending on portion size

INGREDIENTS

Pork shank:

1/4 cup all-purpose flour

Salt and pepper to taste

2-3 pounds fresh pork shank

1/3 cup olive oil

1 cup white wine

Sauce:

1 cup yellow mustard

1/4 cup granulated sugar

1 cup dried apricots

1 cup raisins

3 1/2 cups dry white wine *(preferably Pinot Grigio)*

DIRECTIONS:

Preheat oven to 300° Fahrenheit.

For the pork shank: Mix flour, salt, and pepper together; generously dust the pork with it on all sides. Place sauté pan or heavy skillet over medium-high heat and add the oil. Sear the meat on all sides. Once seared, deglaze the pan with the white wine, scraping to loosen the browned bits from the bottom of the pan. Let the alcohol burn off and place the pan in the oven. Cook until the meat is tender; cooking time depends on how big the shanks are, approximately 20 minutes per pound or until the internal temperature reaches 160° with a meat thermometer. Remove from the oven and place on a warm platter.

For the sauce: Add sauce ingredients to a saucepan or pot. Using a whisk, mix ingredients and heat on medium-low until liquid is reduced by half. Remove from heat, strain the liquid, and place the raisin-apricot mixture in a blender. Blend well for a minute or so. Combine the purée and the liquid with a whisk, and cool the mixture down. Set aside.

To serve: Spoon the warm sauce over the pork.

Ted's Souvlakia

TED'S RESTAURANT

328 12th Street South
Birmingham, Alabama 35233
205-324-2911 | TedsBirmingham.com

ESTABLISHED: 1973

KNOWN FOR: Meat-and-three, a longstanding Birmingham lunch tradition. Ted's offers home-cooked versions of southern comfort food and Greek classics, and they even manage to get you in and out for lunch in 30 minutes! Tasos and Beba, Ted's owners since 2000, greet every customer, and Tasos often gives newcomers one of his special, homemade chocolate chip cookies.

DON'T MISS: Ted's original Pork Souvlakia, a traditional dish served in Greece, prepared with pork, lamb, or beef with Greek seasoning and served on a stick. The cornbread is made from scratch each day, and so are all of the veggies and side dishes served on the steam table. Do not miss Ted's Baklava, layers of phyllo pastry and nuts held together with honey syrup; the recipe is found in *Birmingham's Best Bites* cookbook.

DOWNTOWN

TED'S SOUVLAKIA

Yield: Serves 4-6, depending on portion size

INGREDIENTS

2 pounds pork, lamb, or beef, *cut into 1/2-inch cubes*

1/3 cup olive oil

Juice of 1 lemon

2 teaspoons dried oregano

1 teaspoon garlic powder

Salt and pepper to taste

Skewers

Parsley and lemon wedges for garnish

DIRECTIONS:

Place the meat in a glass dish or in a plastic zip-top bag. Whisk together the olive oil, lemon juice, and spices to combine. Pour over the meat; toss well to coat, and cover with plastic wrap. Marinate in the refrigerator for 12-24 hours, turning the meat occasionally.

Take the meat out of the marinade and thread onto skewers. Cook on a hot grill pan or grill, turning and basting frequently with marinade, for 15 minutes or until cooked to the desired degree of doneness. Place the skewers on a platter and garnish with parsley and lemon wedges.

Notes

GIUSEPPE'S CAFÉ

925 8th Street South
Birmingham, Alabama 35205
205-324-2626 | GiuseppesCafe.com

ESTABLISHED: 2002

KNOWN FOR: Homemade Italian favorites like baked ziti, pizza, manicotti, lasagna, and spaghetti. Students from Birmingham-Southern College have long made the trek to Southside for the Chicken Caesar sub and continue the tradition even after they graduate. Lunch specials are available each day, and it is a popular spot with UAB personnel and students.

DON'T MISS: The Seven Vegetable Penne with creamy feta sauce. The bread at Giuseppe's is baked in-house, and the garlic bread is served buttery and hot. Save room for the desserts; their tiramisu, Italian Crème cake, and cannoli are all made from scratch.

Giuseppe's Chicken and Prosuitto Pasta

SOUTHSIDE

GIUSEPPE'S CHICKEN and PROSCIUTTO PASTA

Yield: 1 serving

INGREDIENTS

1/2 pound penne pasta

1 1/2 tablespoons olive oil

1/3 cup red onion, *diced*

1/2 cup cooked chicken breast, *diced*

1/3 cup prosciutto, *thinly sliced and cut into strips*

1 teaspoon garlic, *minced*

2/3 cup heavy cream

1/3 cup half-and-half

10 medium-sized basil leaves, *chiffonade*

1/2 cup finely grated Parmesan cheese

Salt and pepper to taste

DIRECTIONS:

Cook the penne according to package directions. Set aside.

In medium saucepan, heat the olive oil. Sauté the onion, chicken, and prosciutto until onions are tender. Add the garlic and sauté for 1 minute longer.

Add the cream, half-and-half, basil leaves, and penne pasta; let cook for a minute and a half, stirring constantly. Add Parmesan. Reduce the heat, and continue to cook and reduce until the sauce becomes thick. Add salt and pepper to taste.

Notes

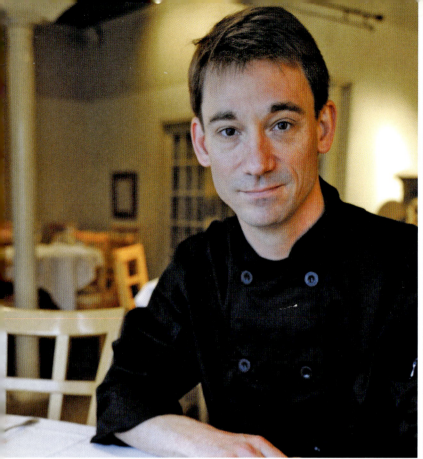

dg

2837 Culver Road
Mountain Brook, Alabama 35223
205-871-3266 | DanielGeorgeRestaurant.com

ESTABLISHED: 2000

KNOWN FOR: Fresh Gulf seafood, wild game, and fresh local produce. Chef Daniel Briggs' menu changes daily based on what comes in the door. Pork Picatta dg has been a favorite since the doors opened. Hearty menu favorites include perfectly prepared Colorado lamb chops, but Chef Briggs is equally adept with delicate scallops.

DON'T MISS: Meat-and-three lunch favorites that include fried chicken with sawmill gravy, hamburger steaks, and lots of fresh veggie side dishes, both modern and traditional. The meat-and-three is served with homemade warm biscuits. Sigh.

Pork Picatta dg

MOUNTAIN BROOK VILLAGE

PORK PICATTA DG

Yield: Serves 4

INGREDIENTS

2 pork tenderloins, *cleaned of silver skin and cut into 2-ounce portions*

1/2 cup canola oil

2 cups all-purpose flour, *seasoned with salt and pepper*

Salt and pepper to taste

3 tablespoons capers

2 tablespoons shallots, *minced*

1/2 cup fresh-squeezed lemon juice

1 cup dry white wine

1 cup unsalted butter

1 tablespoon fresh parsley, *chopped, for garnish*

DIRECTIONS:

Place each portion of pork between 2 sheets of wax paper or 2 freezer bags. Lightly pound each portion to 1/4-inch thickness with a mallet. Add the oil to a sauté pan and heat over medium heat.

Distribute the seasoned flour on a sheet pan. Season the pork with salt and pepper and dredge on one side in the seasoned flour; sauté both sides for 2 minutes per side.

Empty the oil from pan and add the shallots and capers to pan. Deglaze the pan with lemon juice and white wine, stirring constantly to remove the fonds (the brown bits on the bottom of the pan). Cook and reduce by half. Lower the heat and rapidly whisk in the butter, 1 ounce at a time, until it is incorporated before adding the next addition. Continue until all the butter is incorporated, and the sauce thickens. When ready to serve, ladle the sauce over the meat. Garnish with fresh parsley.

Notes

NABEEL'S CAFÉ & MARKET

1706 Oxmoor Road
Homewood, Alabama 35209
205-879-9292 | Nabeels.com

ESTABLISHED: 1972

KNOWN FOR: Homemade Greek and Italian specialties like Moussaka, a sort of Greek lasagna named to the Alabama Tourism Department's list of 100 Dishes to Eat in Alabama Before You Die. During certain holidays like Christmas or Greek Easter, Nabeel's serves its legendary roast leg of lamb with potatoes. It's been a tradition for decades in some families.

DON'T MISS: Avgolemono, a Greek soup made with chicken broth, orzo pasta, lemon, and egg and served with a slice of warm homemade bread. For dessert, try the homemade cannoli stuffed with mascarpone, chocolate chips, and nut cream.

Nabeel's Moussaka

HOMEWOOD

NABEEL'S MOUSSAKA

Yield: 12-15 pieces

INGREDIENTS

1 1/2 large white onions, *minced*

1 cup extra-virgin olive oil, *divided*

2 1/2 pounds lean ground beef

3 cups tomato sauce *(canned or homemade)*

Salt and pepper to taste

1 1/2 cups Parmesan cheese, *shredded, divided*

1/2 cup unsalted butter, *melted*

1 cup all-purpose flour

3 medium eggplant, *sliced 1/4-inch thick*

1 tablespoon ground nutmeg

1 tablespoon ground cinnamon

Béchamel Sauce:

6 tablespoons unsalted butter

6 tablespoons all-purpose flour

1 quart whole milk

1 teaspoon kosher salt

2 eggs

DIRECTIONS:

Preheat oven to 350° Fahrenheit

In a large skillet, sauté the onions in 2 tablespoons olive oil until translucent. Reserve the remaining olive oil for assembly. Add the beef and brown. Add the tomato sauce, salt and pepper, and mix well. Simmer for about 20-25 minutes. Remove meat mixture from the heat and drain excess oil. Stir in 1/2 cup Parmesan cheese. Set aside.

Set up a breading station with the melted butter and the flour in shallow containers. Dip the sliced eggplant in the melted butter and then dredge it in the flour. Shake off the excess. Heat stovetop grill or grill pan and brush with olive oil. Grill eggplant until browned, about 2 minutes per side. Set aside.

For the Béchamel: In a heavy saucepan, melt butter over medium heat. Stir in the flour. Cook, stirring until the mixture starts bubbling. Remove from heat and stir the milk into the flour mixture, using a whisk. Return to medium heat and cook, stirring constantly. Reduce the heat and continue cooking for about 5 minutes, constantly stirring. At this time, the sauce should be very thick. Beat the eggs in a bowl. Add a large spoonful of the hot Béchamel into the eggs, which will temper them. Then quickly add the warmed egg mixture into the sauce, whisking to incorporate fully.

To assemble: Sprinkle remaining olive oil, about 1-2 tablespoons, on the bottom of a 17x11-inch baking pan. Place a layer of the eggplant slices on the bottom. Add a layer of the meat. Repeat this process 2 more times, ending with eggplant. Pour the Béchamel sauce over the top and spread well to cover the entire surface. Sprinkle with nutmeg, cinnamon, salt, pepper, and remaining 1 cup Parmesan cheese. Bake for 45 minutes or until golden brown. Let dish cool for 20 minutes before slicing. Cut into squares to serve.

Desserts

Steel City Pops
▸▸ Coconut Popsicle 194

Niki's West
▸▸ Niki's Famous Banana Pudding 196

Olexa's
▸▸ Carrot Cake with Cream Cheese Icing 198

Full Moon Bar-B-Que
▸▸ Half Moon Cookies 200

Birmingham Breadworks
▸▸ Hummingbird Cake 202

Big Spoon Creamery
▸▸ Fig and Goat Cheese Ice Cream 204

Yo' Mama's Restaurant
▸▸ Peach Cobbler 206

Dreamcakes Bakery
▸▸ Petite Fudge Cakes 208

Rusty's Bar-B-Q
▸▸ Coconut Cream Pie 210

Iz Café
▸▸ Chocolate Mousse Bombes 212

Pie Lab
▸▸ Double Crust Apple Pie 216

Z's Restaurant
▸▸ Sweet Potato Pie 218

Roberts Cuisine
▸▸ Apple Spice Walnut Cake 220

STEEL CITY POPS

Homewood
2821 Central Avenue, Suite 109
Homewood, Alabama 35209
205-803-6502 | SteelCityPops.com

Greystone
5449 Highway 280
Birmingham, Alabama 35242
205-506-2828 | SteelCityPops.com

The Summit
329 Summit Boulevard
Birmingham, Alabama 35243
205-506-2898 | SteelCityPops.com

ESTABLISHED: 2012

KNOWN FOR: Luxury popsicles made from all-natural and local ingredients with addictive fresh fruit and creamy flavors. A family business started in Homewood by Jim Watkins, a man with a passion for his craft, Steel City Pops can now be found in cities around the South, and there's always a line, even in the cold weather months.

DON'T MISS: The Buttermilk Popsicle. It has a cult following that spans generations. Try the Hibiscus or the Strawberry Lemonade if you like a fruity pop, or go with a creamy classic like Vanilla Bean or Coffee. If you like bold flavor, the Maple Bacon with Bourbon may be your jam. Flavors are seasonal and change weekly; be adventurous and try them all!

Steel City's Coconut Popsicle

LOCAL CHAIN

STEEL CITY'S COCONUT POPSICLE

Yield: 6-8 regular-sized popsicles

INGREDIENTS

2 cups organic cane sugar

2 cups water

2 cups coconut milk

1/2 cup unsweetened organic coconut

1 cup heavy cream

Dash kosher salt

1/4 cup unsweetened coconut, *toasted*

DIRECTIONS:

For the simple syrup: Combine organic cane sugar and water in a saucepan. Stir. Bring to a boil and immediately remove from the heat. Stir to ensure sugar is dissolved and allow to cool completely.

For the pop: In a saucepan bring coconut milk, coconut, and heavy cream to a simmer for 10 minutes. Remove from heat, add salt, and let mixture sit in the refrigerator overnight until coconut flavor is infused into cream.

To freeze: Strain off the raw coconut from the creamy mixture and add simple syrup. Stir in toasted coconut. Place in molds and freeze for at least 8 hours until firm. Unmold and enjoy.

Notes

NIKI'S WEST

233 Finley Avenue West
Birmingham, Alabama 35204
205-252-5751 | NikisWest.com

ESTABLISHED: 1957 by the Hozantas family.

KNOWN FOR: Family tradition. Current owners, Gus Hontzas' sons Pete and Teddy Hontzas, are always greeting guests or serving diners on the line. They have maintained the old-school traditions and recipes their father established and are now passing down these traditions to their own children. The steam-table menu is updated daily with specials that include baked Greek chicken, roast lamb with mint jelly, and country fried steak, along with an a la carte menu for steaks and seafood.

DON'T MISS: The seafood specialties. These include Fresh Baked Snapper a la Niki's. The breakfast menu is full of home-cooked favorites like fluffy made-from-scratch biscuits, omelets, and eggs cooked the way you like them. The cinnamon rolls are legendary, too. When you order from the menu, they will bring a basket to you. The one recipe everyone begs for is Niki's banana pudding. Served warm, it has been on the menu and made by Miss Hudson as long as anyone can remember.

Niki's Famous Banana Pudding

NIKI'S FAMOUS BANANA PUDDING

Yield: Serves 10-12, depending on portion size

INGREDIENTS

1 3/4 cups granulated sugar

3/4 cup all-purpose flour

2 3/4 cups milk

4 egg yolks *(Save the whites for the meringue.)*

2 tablespoons vanilla extract

1 (11-ounce) box Nilla® Wafers

3 ripe bananas, *cut into 1/4-inch-thick slices (approximately 3 cups)*

Meringue:

1/4 cup granulated sugar

4 egg whites

1/4 teaspoon vanilla extract

DIRECTIONS:

Preheat oven to 400° Fahrenheit.

Whisk together 1 3/4 cups sugar and flour in a medium-size heavy saucepan. Gradually whisk in milk until blended. Cook over medium heat, whisking constantly, 5 minutes or until thickened.

In a separate bowl, whisk egg yolks until thick and pale. Gradually whisk about 1/4 of hot milk mixture into yolks. Add the tempered yolk mixture to remaining hot milk mixture, whisking constantly. Return the mixture to the saucepan and cook over low heat, whisking constantly, 5 minutes or until thickened. Remove from heat. Stir in 2 tablespoons vanilla. Toss together vanilla wafers and banana slices in an 11-by-7-inch baking dish. Top with the warm pudding.

For the meringue: Beat egg whites at high speed with an electric mixer until foamy. Gradually add 1/4 cup sugar, 1 tablespoon at a time, beating until stiff peaks form and sugar dissolves, about 2 to 4 minutes. Beat in 1/4 teaspoon vanilla with the last tablespoon of sugar. Spread meringue over warm pudding, making sure to seal the meringue at the edges of dish.

Bake pudding at 400° for 8 minutes or until golden brown. Let stand 30 minutes before serving. Serve warm.

Note: For a less sweet custard, reduce the amount of sugar in the custard by 1/4 cup and reduce the vanilla from 2 tablespoons to 1.

ACIPCO-FINLEY

Olexa's Carrot Cake with Cream Cheese Icing

OLEXA'S

2838 Culver Road
Mountain Brook, Alabama 35223
205-871-2060 | Olexas.com

ESTABLISHED: 2004

KNOWN FOR: Magnificent wedding cakes, designed by owner Diane Olexa. At the restaurant, Diane serves her cake (chocolate fudge or French vanilla) slightly warm with an extra dollop of her equally famed buttercream on the side. You'll also find toasty paninis, a wide variety of fresh salads, crepes, and homemade soups there. Olexa's is extremely popular for birthdays, bridesmaid luncheons, and new baby celebrations. We asked Diane to give us her most popular "make-at-home" cake creation. This recipe is her mother's that they have made for more than 45 years.

DON'T MISS: The Tomato Basil Bisque. It may have as much of a fan following as Diane's wedding cakes. It is so popular that diners can now purchase quarts of soup to-go. Ask about the Cloud Nine: buttercream cake, fresh strawberries, and whipping cream.

MOUNTAIN BROOK VILLAGE

OLEXA'S CARROT CAKE with CREAM CHEESE ICING

Yield: 1 9-inch (2-layer) cake

INGREDIENTS

2 cups all-purpose flour

2 teaspoons baking soda

2 teaspoons ground cinnamon

1 teaspoon salt

3 large eggs

3/4 cup vegetable oil

3/4 cup whole buttermilk

2 cups granulated sugar

2 teaspoons pure vanilla extract

1 (8-ounce) can crushed pineapple, with juice

1 cup sweetened coconut *(Olexa's recommends Baker's Angel Flake.)*

1/2 cup golden raisins

1/2 cup brown raisins

1 cup walnuts, *chopped*

3 cups carrots, *grated*

Cream Cheese Icing:

1/4 pound unsalted butter, *softened to room temperature*

1 (8-ounce) block Philadelphia Cream Cheese, *softened to room temperature*

1 teaspoon pure almond extract

1-pound Confectioners sugar

1 teaspoon milk or heavy cream, *if needed*

DIRECTIONS:

Preheat oven to 350° Fahrenheit. Lightly grease and flour two 9-inch round layer pans.

Sift the flour, baking soda, cinnamon, and salt together into a large bowl. In a separate bowl, beat the eggs, oil, buttermilk, sugar, and vanilla together and mix well. Add the dry ingredients to the batter. In a separate bowl, mix the pineapple, coconut, raisins, nuts, and carrots together, and carefully fold the mixture into the batter. Pour the completed batter into the prepared pans.

Bake at 350° Fahrenheit for 30-35 minutes or until a cake tester inserted into the center comes out clean with only a few moist crumbs sticking to it. Baking time will differ based on pan size and type.

Allow the cakes to cool completely before icing. If you're using round layer pans, remove the layers from the pans after 15 minutes and place them on a rack to cool.

For the icing: Using a mixer, beat the butter and cream cheese together until smooth. Add the almond extract. Reduce speed to low, and add the Confectioners sugar, a little at a time until it is all incorporated. Add a teaspoon of milk or heavy cream to the icing if it is too stiff to spread. You may also add additional sugar if it is thin.

To assemble: Use an offset spatula to ice the top of one layer; top with the second layer, and ice the top and sides of the cake.

Full Moon Bar-B-Que's Half Moon Cookies

FULL MOON BAR-B-QUE

Southside | Homewood | Hoover | Inverness
Alabaster | UAB
FullMoonBBQ.com

ESTABLISHED: 1986

KNOWN FOR: Authentic barbecue, southern style, which they cook low and slow over hickory wood. Full Moon has long claimed the title of "The Best Little Pork House in Alabama." While they specialize in pork, ribs, and Boston butts, it is their beef brisket that many say is the best in Birmingham. In 2013, Full Moon was named one of the top 10 barbecue restaurants in the entire USA by the *Huffington Post*. Their brisket recipe is featured in *Birmingham's Best Bites*.

DON'T MISS: The spicy sweet chow-chow relish. The Full Moon slaw, along with these oh-so-popular Half Moon Cookies, is found on the Alabama Department of Tourism's list of 100 Dishes to Eat in Alabama Before You Die. If you're not a baker, you can order a tin of can't-eat-just-one Half-Moon Cookies to ship anywhere in the US. Save room for pie, too!

LOCAL CHAIN

FULL MOON BAR-B-QUE'S HALF MOON COOKIES

Yield: About 4 dozen

INGREDIENTS

Cookie:

2 1/4 cups all-purpose flour, *unsifted*

1 teaspoon baking soda

1 teaspoon salt

1/2 pound butter, *softened*

3/4 cup granulated sugar

3/4 cup light brown sugar, *packed*

2 large eggs

1 teaspoon pure vanilla extract

3 cups semi-sweet chocolate chips

1 cup pecans, *chopped*

Milk Chocolate Dip:

1 pound Hershey bar, *chopped*

DIRECTIONS:

Preheat oven to 375° Fahrenheit.

For the cookie: Combine flour, baking soda, and salt in a medium bowl and set aside. Cream together butter, granulated sugar, and brown sugar in a large bowl. Beat in eggs and vanilla. Slowly add the dry ingredients until blended, and then stir in the chocolate chips and pecans.

Use a rounded teaspoon to scoop out dough and drop onto an ungreased cookie sheet.

Bake 8-10 minutes. Cool cookies on a rack and refrigerate.

For the chocolate dip: Melt Hershey bar slowly. Take cookie after it has been refrigerated and dip half of it into the melted chocolate. Set on a cold sheet pan to cool.

Notes

Hummingbird Cake

BIRMINGHAM BREADWORKS

2408 7th Avenue South
Birmingham, Alabama 35233
205-933-7517 | BirminghamBreadworks.com

ESTABLISHED: 2014

KNOWN FOR: Fresh, made-from-scratch baked goods, breads, and pastries, including French baguettes, ham and cheese croissants, chocolate croissants, almond croissants, and cream cheese Danish. Sandwiches such as Vulcan's Veggie, made with portobella mushrooms, spinach, and mozzarella on their own freshly baked bread, make the bakery a popular lunch destination on the Southside and one of the few places you can get a homemade breakfast during the week.

DON'T MISS: The pizza, which changes daily, and the cinnamon rolls. Order your next birthday cake here; the Hummingbird Cake is the house favorite and you can get it by the slice when it is on the menu.

HUMMINGBIRD CAKE

Yield: 1 (3-tier) 9-inch cake

INGREDIENTS

Cake:

1 1/2 cups unsalted butter, *softened, plus more for the pans*

3 cups unbleached all-purpose flour, *plus more for the pans*

2 1/2 teaspoons baking powder

1 1/4 teaspoons kosher salt

3/4 teaspoon baking soda

2 cups very ripe bananas, mashed *(about 5 medium-sized bananas)*

1 (8.25-ounce) can crushed pineapple

1 cup low-fat buttermilk, *at room temperature*

1 3/4 cups light brown sugar, *packed*

4 large eggs, *at room temperature*

1 cup pecans, *chopped*

1 cup sweetened shredded coconut

Frosting:

1 pound cream cheese, *softened*

1 1/2 cups unsalted butter, *softened*

4 cups Confectioners sugar

4 teaspoons pure vanilla extract

3/4 teaspoon salt

DIRECTIONS:

Position a rack in the center of the oven. Preheat the oven to 350° Fahrenheit.

Butter three 9-inch round cake pans, line the bottoms with parchment, butter the parchment, and flour the pans. Tap the pans to remove excess flour. Set aside.

For the cake: In a medium bowl, whisk together the flour, baking powder, salt, and baking soda, and set aside.

In a small bowl, whisk bananas, pineapple, and buttermilk together. Using a stand mixer, cream the butter and sugar until light and fluffy. Add the eggs, one at a time, beating well after each addition. Reduce speed to low and alternately add flour and banana/pineapple mixtures in three additions. Remove the bowl from the stand and fold in the pecans and coconut with a spatula. Divide the batter evenly among the pans and smooth with the spatula. Tap the pans on the counter to break any air bubbles.

Bake, rotating and switching positions halfway through, until a tester inserted in the centers comes out clean, about 30-35 minutes. Let the cakes cool in the pans on baking racks for 10 minutes. Turn the cakes out onto the racks, remove the parchment, and cool completely.

For the frosting: In the large bowl of a stand mixer, beat the cream cheese and butter with the mixer on medium speed until very smooth and creamy, about 1 minute. Add the Confectioners sugar, vanilla, and salt, and beat on medium-high until blended and fluffy, about 2 minutes. Cover the frosting and set aside at room temperature until the layers are completely cool.

To assemble: Set one cake layer upside down on a flat serving plate. Using a metal spatula, evenly spread 1 1/2 cups of the frosting over the top of the layer. Top with the remaining cake layer, so the rounded side is on bottom. Spread a thin layer (about 1/3 cup) of frosting over the entire cake to seal in the crumbs; fill in gaps between the layers. Refrigerate until chilled, about 20 minutes. Spread the entire cake with the remaining frosting.

Refrigerate cake for 2 hours prior to serving. Allow the cake to come to room temperature before cutting. The flavors will improve with time, so you may bake and frost the cake up to two days before you serve it. Refrigerate leftovers.

Photo: Stephen Devries

Big Spoon Fig and Goat Cheese Ice Cream

BIG SPOON CREAMERY

4000 3rd Avenue South, Suite 104
Birmingham, Alabama 35222
205-703-4712 | BigSpoonCreamery.com

ESTABLISHED: 2014

KNOWN FOR: Artisanal small-batch ice cream using seasonal flavors and made with locally sourced ingredients. Husband and wife chefs Geri-Martha and Ryan O'Hara have spun their love of cooking, community, and seasonal ingredients into the best ice cream in the Magic City. Fans drive to find "Bessie Blue," their big blue ice cream truck, or stop by their new brick-and-mortar location in Avondale for scoops in homemade waffle cones or Big Spoon's trademark ice cream "sammies," which sandwich ice cream between two house-baked gourmet cookies.

DON'T MISS: Anything with buttermilk or berries. Flavors change with the seasons, but watch for these key ingredients. In the summer, the Honeysuckle Blackberry is always popular, and the Coffee Almond Toffee is addictive. The caramel is fantastic, especially on the house-made honey graham cookies.

FOOD TRUCK AND AVONDALE

BIG SPOON FIG and GOAT CHEESE ICE CREAM

Yield: 2 quarts

INGREDIENTS

Fig Swirl:

2 pints fresh figs, *cleaned and halved (Big Spoon uses figs from Petals from the Past in Jemison, Alabama.)*

Juice of 1 lemon

1 vanilla bean, *split and seeds scrapped*

1/2 cup granulated sugar

Goat Cheese Ice Cream Base:

6 cups whole milk

1/4 cup heavy cream *(Use 35% cream, if you can find it.)*

1/4 cup non-fat milk powder

3/4 cup dextrose *(You can find dextrose at most grocery stores. Look for it on the sugar or baking aisle. You may substitute 3/4 cup granulated sugar in its place.)*

1 cup granulated sugar

12 egg yolks

Pinch kosher salt

12 ounces Stone Hollow Farmstead goat cheese *(You may substitute a different brand.)*

DIRECTIONS:

For the Fig Swirl: Cook all ingredients in a small saucepan; bring to a simmer and cook for 15 minutes. Remove the vanilla bean and blend using an immersion blender or regular blender. Pour into a container to cool down. Chill in refrigerator until you are ready to swirl into your ice cream.

For the Goat Cheese Ice Cream Base: Pour the milk and cream into a container with twice the capacity of the mixture. While whisking the mixture, add the milk powder. Puree this with an immersion blender or regular blender.

Pour the mixture into a saucepan and heat over medium heat. Once it reaches 104° Fahrenheit, whisk in the dextrose, sugar, and egg yolks. Whisking constantly, heat to 185°. Remove from the heat. Prepare an ice bath using ice and cold water. Submerge the bottom half of the saucepan in the ice bath and whisk a bit to cool the mixture to 40°. Place in a container and refrigerate for 6-12 hours to allow it to mature.

To freeze: Blend in the Stone Hollow Farmstead goat cheese with an immersion blender. Strain. Pour into the ice cream freezer. When the ice cream is almost finished spinning, swirl in the chilled fig purée.

YO' MAMA'S RESTAURANT

2328 2nd Avenue North
Birmingham, Alabama 35203
205-957-6545 | YoMamasRestaurant.com

ESTABLISHED: 2007

KNOWN FOR: Lunch! Yo' Mama's was named best lunch in Birmingham according to a 2016 *Birmingham Magazine* readers' poll. A loyal following lines up for their home-cooked fish, chicken, and soul food favorites. They have quite a few gluten-free offerings, and their popular "POE" (Put on Everything) Sauce is a gluten-free, almond-based recipe.

DON'T MISS: Saturday brunch. Salmon Croquettes, Chicken and Waffles, Shrimp and Grits, French Toast, and Belgian Waffles with a peach cobbler topping are the big favorites. Plan ahead; they only serve brunch on the second and last Saturdays of each month.

Yo' Mama's Peach Cobbler

YO' MAMA'S PEACH COBBLER

Yield: 1 cobbler

INGREDIENTS

Filling:

4 cups sliced peaches *(fresh or frozen)*

1 1/2 cups granulated sugar

1 cup water

1 stick butter

1 teaspoon vanilla extract

1/2 teaspoon lemon extract

1 teaspoon ground cinnamon

1/2 teaspoon ground nutmeg

Crust:

1 1/2 cups self-rising flour

1/2 teaspoon baking powder

1/4 teaspoon ground cinnamon

1 stick butter

3/4 cup ice water

Cinnamon to taste

Granulated sugar to taste

DIRECTIONS:

Preheat oven 375° Fahrenheit.

For the filling: Combine all filling ingredients in saucepan. Bring to a boil medium to medium-high heat and let it cook for 15 minutes.

Pour in a pie pan or Pyrex dish.

For the crust: Combine flour, baking powder, and cinnamon in medium bowl. Break up butter into small pieces and place in the middle of flour. Combine butter and flour with fork. Pour water into the mixture slowly while stirring with a fork to prevent clumping. Sprinkle cutting board with flour and place dough on cutting board. Spread dough until about 1/4 inch thick. Cut dough into strips and place on top of peach filling. Sprinkle with sugar and cinnamon.

Bake at 375° until crust is done, about 25 minutes.

DREAMCAKES BAKERY

960 Oxmoor Road
Homewood, Alabama 35209
205-871-9377 | Dreamcakes-Bakery.com

ESTABLISHED: 2009

KNOWN FOR: Cupcakes and cakes. Dreamcakes owner, pastry chef, and cookbook author Jan Jacks-Potter started the first cupcake/food truck in Birmingham in 2008. Now, you can get her magical cupcakes at their flagship store in Homewood, from their truck, or at supermarkets around town. Dreamcakes crafts some of the most extraordinary special occasion and wedding cakes you've ever tasted, and they make the cutest cupcakes in pink or blue for gender reveal parties.

DON'T MISS: Anything with caramel icing like the Caramel Sea Salt Mocha. The Honey Lavender cupcakes are completely addictive. If they have strawberry cake, order it! Jacks-Potter's mother made these Petite Fudge Cakes for special occasions when she was a girl. She said not to let their unpretentious appearance fool you. Six simple ingredients transform into a decadent dessert that is irresistible, and the middle becomes a little pocket to hold sweetened whipped cream or ice cream.

(Above) Petite Fudge Cakes (Below) Photo: Karim Shamsi-Basha

HOMEWOOD

PETITE FUDGE CAKES

Yield: 2 dozen

INGREDIENTS

6 (1-ounce) semi-sweet chocolate squares

1 cup unsalted butter

1 3/4 cup granulated sugar

1 cup all-purpose flour

4 large eggs

2 teaspoons vanilla extract

1/4 teaspoon kosher salt

Foil cupcake liners

Whipped cream, ice cream, or a dusting of unsweetened cocoa for garnish

DIRECTIONS:

Preheat oven to 350° Fahrenheit.

Melt chocolate and butter over a double boiler, and let the mixture cool.

In another bowl, combine the sugar, flour, and eggs, stirring with a whisk. Add chocolate mixture; stir until just mixed. Add vanilla and salt.

Scoop the batter into foil-lined muffin pans about 2/3 full. Bake at 350° for 15 minutes. Be careful not to over bake. They should be gooey. (They will crack and sink in the middle; this is normal). Cool and top with sweetened whipped cream or ice cream or simply dust with unsweetened cocoa or powdered sugar.

Note: You can make these cakes in regular or mini-size foil cupcake liners.

Notes

Coconut Cream Pie

RUSTY'S BAR-B-Q

7484 Parkway Drive
Leeds, Alabama 35094
205-699-4766 | RustysBarBQ.com

ESTABLISHED: 2009

KNOWN FOR: Pulled pork and smoked meats. In 2015, Rusty's won the "Mom and Pop" division of the Alabama Department of Tourism's Alabama Barbecue Battle. Using family recipes and skills learned at culinary school, Jonathan Tucker and his wife, Beth, have made Leeds a mecca for barbecue aficionados. Rusty's is also known for house-made barbecue sauces and a mean burger that has a huge fan following.

DON'T MISS: The smoked meats, of course, but save room for the homemade desserts. Rusty's has the traditional cream pies typically found at most barbecue joints, but also offers seasonal desserts and dessert specials. If you are lucky enough to go when there is Italian Crème Cake on the menu, get a whole one to take home. Call before you go to make sure they have your favorite on the menu that day, or you can order in advance. Most requested is the Coconut Cream Pie made from Rusty's grandfather's recipe.

COCONUT CREAM PIE

Yield: 1 pie

INGREDIENTS

1 pie shell shell (store-bought)

Filling:

3/4 cup granulated sugar

1 can coconut milk

1/4 cup cornstarch

1/2 cup whole milk

1/2 teaspoon vanilla

3 egg yolks

1/4 stick (1/8 cup) unsalted butter

1/2 cup shredded unsweetened coconut, plus additional 1/4 cup for garnish

Italian Meringue:

1/2 cup granulated sugar

1/4 cup water

2 egg whites

1/2 teaspoon cream of tartar

Pinch salt

DIRECTIONS:

Note: You may make the filling a day ahead and complete the meringue just prior to serving.

Preheat the oven to the temperature indicated on the crust package or recipe.

Dock (prick) the pie shell with a fork and blind bake until golden brown. (Follow the package instructions; some suggest filling the shell with pie weights, uncooked dried beans, or uncooked rice.)

After the pie crust is browned, spread 1/4 cup of the coconut on a sheet pan and lightly toast until golden brown. Set aside. (Note: Watch carefully because it burns easily!)

For the filling: Combine sugar, cornstarch, coconut milk, whole milk, and vanilla in a heavy saucepan. Whisk to combine. Cook on stove until the mixture reaches 180° Fahrenheit using a candy thermometer.

Off the heat, use a ladle to add some of the egg to the hot milk mixture, whisking to temper the yolks. Gradually whisk in all the egg and then return the egg/milk mixture to the pot. Cook over medium-high heat, stirring constantly with a rubber spatula to prevent sticking. As the mixture starts to thicken, whisk in butter and turn off heat. The mixture should be the consistency of pudding. Whisk until smooth. Stir in the coconut.

Pour mixture into pie shell and chill in the refrigerator until the filling has set up, at least 2 hours.

For the meringue: Use a stand mixer with a whisk attachment to beat the egg whites, salt, and cream of tartar at medium speed. At the same time, combine the sugar and water in a saucepan. Using a candy thermometer, cook the sugar syrup until it reaches 235°. Remove from the heat.

The egg whites should be at medium peaks. Increase the speed of the stand mixer to high and slowly drizzle in the hot syrup between the whisk and the side of the bowl. The mixture should build into a fluffy meringue. Top the pie with the meringue. Brown the top of the pie using a kitchen torch or your oven's broiler setting. Top with toasted coconut.

Chocolate Mousse Bombes

IZ CAFÉ

IZ CAFÉ ORIGINAL
2514 Rocky Ridge Road
Vestavia Hills, Alabama 35243
205-979-7570 | EverythingIz.com

ESTABLISHED: 1999

KNOWN FOR: Lunch favorites. The Vestavia Hills/Rocky Ridge. café is a favorite for soups, salads, sandwiches, wraps, and celebrated house-made desserts. You can always get-it-to-go with their assortment of pre-cooked specials available daily. Tuesday and Thursday are take-home Chicken Pot Pie nights; other weeknight specials include pot roast, salmon cakes, or chicken and dumplings.

DON'T MISS: The Iz Chicken Salad, their signature recipe that helped create the Iz food empire. Also try the roast beef sandwich: slow braised beef, Provolone, crispy onions, and gravy. These Chocolate Mousse Bombes are the most popular dessert, but many others keep guests coming back. Kay Bruno Reed and her team have been making hungry people happy for a long time. Now you can even find her Iz Good Stuff products at local supermarkets.

VESTAVIA HILLS

CHOCOLATE MOUSSE BOMBES

DEVIL'S FOOD CAKE TOPPED WITH CHOCOLATE MOUSSE DIPPED IN CHOCOLATE GANACHE
Yield: 24 pieces

INGREDIENTS

Devil's Food Cake:

3/4 cup Dutch-processed cocoa powder, *plus more for pans*

1/2 cup boiling water

1 1/2 cups (3 sticks) unsalted butter, *plus more for pans*

2 1/4 cups granulated sugar

1 tablespoon pure vanilla extract

4 large eggs, *lightly beaten*

3 cups sifted cake flour (not self-rising)

1 teaspoon baking soda

1/2 teaspoon salt

1 cup milk

Chocolate Mousse:

1 quart heavy cream

1/2 cup granulated sugar

6 ounces coffee, at room temperature

6 egg yolks

1 pound semi-sweet chocolate

Ganache:

1 quart heavy cream

2 pounds semi-sweet chocolate

Special equipment:

Non-stick silicone sphere mold

DIRECTIONS:

Preheat the oven to 350° Fahrenheit. Arrange two racks in the center of oven.

For the cake: Butter 2 rimmed 18x13-inch baking sheets; line bottoms with parchment paper. Dust bottoms and sides of sheets with cocoa powder; tap out any excess.

Sift cocoa into a medium, heat-proof bowl, and whisk in boiling water. Set aside to cool.

In the bowl of an electric mixer, fitted with the paddle attachment, cream 3 sticks butter on low speed until light and fluffy. Gradually beat in the sugar until light and fluffy, about 3-4 minutes, scraping down sides twice. Beat in vanilla. Drizzle in eggs, a little at a time, beating between each addition until the batter is no longer slick, scraping down the sides twice.

In a large bowl, sift together flour, baking soda, and salt.

CHOCOLATE MOUSSE BOMBES

(continued)

Whisk milk into reserved cocoa mixture. With the mixer on low speed, alternately add the flour and cocoa mixtures to the batter, a little of each at a time, starting and ending with flour mixture.

Divide batter evenly among the prepared pans. Bake until a cake tester inserted into center of each layer comes out clean, about 25-30 minutes, rotating the pans for even baking. Transfer layers to wire racks; let cool for 15 minutes. Turn out cakes, and return to racks, tops up, until completely cool.

Take a 2 1/2-inch cookie cutter, and cut cake into 24 pieces. Set aside.

For the mousse: Beat heavy cream until stiff peaks form. Cover and chill.

Combine sugar into coffee; slowly add the yolks set over a saucepan of gently simmering water (do not allow bowl to touch water). Cook the mixture, whisking constantly, until it has almost doubled in volume and an instant read thermometer inserted into the mixture registers 160°, about 1-2 minutes.

Remove the bowl from pan. Add chocolate, and whisk until melted and smooth. Whisking occasionally, let stand until room temperature.

Fold heavy cream into chocolate mixture and chill.

For the ganache: Heat heavy cream just enough to melt the chocolate; do not simmer or boil. Pour cream over chocolate and stir until melted.

Assembly: Use a non-stick silicone sphere mold. Scoop the mousse into mold. Top with chocolate cake round and freeze until firm. Remove frozen cake and mousse from mold and dip in the ganache. Place on a parchment-paper lined baking sheet. Chill until ready to serve.

PIE LAB

2829 2nd Avenue South
Birmingham, AL 35233
pepperplacemarket.com

1317 Main Street
Greensboro, Alabama 36744
334-624-3899

ESTABLISHED: 2009 in Greensboro, Alabama. Pie Lab makes a weekly appearance at The Market at Pepper Place with hundreds of homemade pies for their legions of Birmingham fans. Their restaurant in Greensboro offers daily menu and lunch specials.

KNOWN FOR: Homemade pies of all kinds. Favorites include Chocolate Bourbon Pecan, Brown Sugar Buttermilk, Lemon Chess, and Apple, which won an award from *Garden & Gun* magazine as one of the best pies in the South. The Double Crust Apple Pie is made with Empire apples, which mature in September and October.

DON'T MISS: The Cutie Pies, 6-inch versions of their standard 9-inch pies in all of their most popular flavors; you can also buy them at Black Sheep Kitchen in Crestline Village. Check out their new "Take and Bake" casseroles. Baked Spaghetti, Chicken Florentine, Hash Brown Casserole, and others serve 3-4 and are ready to bake when you need something fast.

Pie Lab Double Crust Apple Pie

(Below) Photo: Erin Snell

PIE LAB DOUBLE CRUST APPLE PIE

Yield: 6-8 slices for a 9-inch pie

INGREDIENTS

1 large egg yolk

1 tablespoon heavy cream

2 tablespoons fresh lemon juice

1/4 cup raw cane sugar, *plus extra for sprinkling*

1/4 cup all-purpose flour

1/8 teaspoon ground cinnamon

1/4 teaspoon ground nutmeg

1/4 teaspoon kosher salt

3 pounds Empire apples, *peeled and sliced*

1 tablespoon unsalted butter

1/2 cup toasted pecans

2 (9-inch) pie crusts *(You may use store-bought or make your own.)*

Heavy cream, whipped, or cranberry sauce for garnish

DIRECTIONS:

Preheat oven to 350° Fahrenheit.

In a small bowl, whisk the egg yolk and cream for the egg wash. Set aside.

Mix lemon juice, sugar, flour, cinnamon, nutmeg, and salt in a large bowl. Add in apple slices and toss to coat. Dot with butter. Fold in pecans.

Place a pastry crust in a 9-inch pie dish. Add the filling. Top with second shell and crimp edges to seal, removing excess dough. Brush top shell with egg wash, sprinkle with the reserved sugar, and cut several small slits to ventilate.

Bake 35 to 45 minutes, or until crust is golden brown. Serve warm with a generous drizzle of heavy cream and a dollop of whole cranberry sauce if you like.

Z's Sweet Potato Pie

Z'S RESTAURANT

104 17th Street North
Birmingham, Alabama 35203
205-250-6288 | zs-restaurant.weebly.com

ESTABLISHED: August 8, 2008, by owner Zeke Hameen on his 74th birthday

KNOWN FOR: The pies. Z's homemade Vanilla Bean Pie was made famous when it was featured on the Travel Channel's *Bizarre Food America* with Andrew Zimmern. They sell 40 to 50 pies a week, and the Sweet Potato Pie is always a holiday favorite. Whether you eat in or call ahead for pick-up, you'll always find Zeke behind the counter, and he'll make sure you leave with a piece of pie.

DON'T MISS: The baked chicken and their fresh collard greens (recipe is featured in *Birmingham's Best Bites*). People line up for the Baked Spaghetti with two sides on Monday and the Baked Chicken and Dressing special on Wednesday. If you love liver, Z's is one of the few places in town you can still get it. Specials change, so call ahead to make sure what you want is available before you go. On Sunday, most of their specials can be found on their lavish buffet (a bargain at only $12), but go early so you don't miss out.

DOWNTOWN

Z's SWEET POTATO PIE

Yield: 1 (9-inch) pie

INGREDIENTS

3 medium sweet potatoes

1/2 stick unsalted butter, *at room temperature*

1 cup granulated sugar

1 teaspoon vanilla extract

2 eggs, *at room temperature*

1/4 cup evaporated milk

1 tablespoon ground cinnamon

1/2 tablespoon ground nutmeg

1/4 teaspoon baking powder

2 tablespoons all-purpose flour, *sifted*

1 frozen pie crust

Whipped cream for garnish

DIRECTIONS:

Preheat oven to 400° Fahrenheit.

Place potatoes in a deep, well-greased pan and bake until entirely cooked. You can test to see if the potatoes are done by sticking a knife into them. If the blade goes all the way through to the pan, they are done. When potatoes are thoroughly cooked, remove the skin. Cut into pieces.

Place potato pieces into a large bowl of an electric mixer. Beat on medium speed until smooth. Slowly add butter, sugar, and vanilla. Reduce the speed and add eggs, one at a time. Pour in evaporated milk, cinnamon, nutmeg, baking powder, and flour. Continue beating on medium speed until the batter is thick and smooth.

Pour the mixture into a thawed or partially frozen pie crust. Reduce the oven temperature to 350°. Bake for 45-50 minutes until set and a toothpick comes out clean. Allow to cool before serving; add a dollop of whipped cream if desired.

Notes

Apple Spice Walnut Cake

ROBERTS CUISINE

10 6th Avenue South
Birmingham AL 35205
205-918-0356 | RobertsCuisine.com

ESTABLISHED: Catering Business 1996, Restaurant 1995

KNOWN FOR: Soul food favorites like Chicken and Waffles, which was featured in *Birmingham's Best Bites*. Other favorites include catfish and grits, and Smoked Turkey Legs. The Braised Beef Oxtails has a loyal following; Roberts is one of the few restaurants in Birmingham serving them. Primarily a catering company, Roberts is only open from 11 a.m.-3 p.m. each Sunday for brunch.

DON'T MISS: Broccoli Rice Casserole like your mama makes and Cajun Maque Choux like you rarely find outside of Louisiana. If you don't have room for dessert, make sure to take home some Strawberry Cake for later!

APPLE SPICE WALNUT CAKE
(Or Mini Bundt Cakes)

Yield: 1 Bundt cake or 12 mini Bundt cakes

INGREDIENTS

2 cups granulated sugar
1 tablespoon ground cinnamon
3 eggs, *beaten*
1 cup vegetable oil
2 1/2 cups self-rising flour
3 cups apple, *chopped*
1 1/2 cups walnuts, *chopped*
Non-stick cooking spray

Glaze:
1 cup dark brown sugar
1/4 cup (1/2 stick) margarine
1 teaspoon ground cinnamon
1 cup fat-free evaporated milk

DIRECTIONS:

Preheat oven to 350° Fahrenheit.

In the bowl of your mixer, combine sugar and cinnamon. Add eggs and oil; beat until fluffy. Turn down the speed and slowly add flour, a little at a time. Carefully fold in the apples and walnuts.

Spray a Bundt pan or mini Bundt pans with non-stick spray. Add the batter, filling 3/4 full. Bake at 350° until toothpick inserted in the center comes out clean, approximately 52-54 minutes for the cake and 8-20 minutes for mini cakes.

Allow the cake to cool in the pan for 10-12 minutes. Turn out onto cooling rack. Glaze while the cake is still warm.

For the glaze: Add all glaze ingredients to a saucepan. Cook over low heat until it comes to a rapid boil. Boil 1 minute. Remove from heat. Allow to cool to warm and pour over the cake while it is still warm.

Notes

index...
RESTAURANTS

5 Point Public House, **138**

Ashley Mac's, **122**

Avo Restaurant, **98**

Bamboo on 2nd, **78**

Big Spoon Creamery, **204**

Birmingham Breadworks, **202**

Blackwell's Pub & Eatery, **176**

Bottega, **84**

Bottega Café, **104**

Brick & Tin, **64, 142**

Busy Corner Cheese & Provisions, **144**

Century Restaurant & Bar, **94**

Chez Fonfon, **80**

Cobb Lane Restaurant, **34**

dg, **188**

Dram Whiskey Bar, **52**

Dreamcakes Bakery, **208**

Dyron's Lowcountry, **58, 128**

Ed Salem's Drive In, **40**

Ensley Grill, **44**

5 Point Public House, **138**

Formosa Hoover Chinese Restaurant, **134**

Full Moon Bar-B-Que, **200**

Gallery Bar, **66**

Gianmarco's Restaurant, **160**

Gilchrist Sandwich Shop, **136**

Giuseppe's Café, **186**

Gulas' Restaurant, **38**

Highlands Bar and Grill, **102**

Holler & Dash, **130**

Homewood Gourmet, **120**

Hot and Hot Fish Club, **112**

Ireland's, **32**

Irondale Café, **118**

Iz Café, **212**

Jim 'N Nick's Bar-B-Q, **164**

Jinsei, **56**

John's City Diner, **68, 110**

John's Restaurant, **30**

Joy Young, **26**

L
Little Savannah Restaurant and Bar, **72, 170**

M
Marsh Bakery, **28**

Miss Dots, **162**

N
Nabeel's Café & Market, **96, 190**

Niki's West, **196**

O
Ocean, **158**

Olexa's, **198**

OvenBird, **116**

P
Pie Lab, **216**

Pioneer Cafeteria, **36**

Post Office Pies, **108**

R
Revelator Coffee, **140**

Rib-It-Up, **92**

Roberts Cuisine, **220**

Roots & Revelry, **74**

Rossi's Italian Restaurant, **42**

Rusty's Bar-B-Q, **210**

S
Satterfield's Restaurant, **180**

Saw's Juke Joint, **62**

Saw's Soul Kitchen, **154**

Shindig's Catering & Food Truck, **148**

Silvertron Café, **182**

Sky Castle Gastro Lounge, **90**

Slice Pizza & Brewhouse, **86**

Snapper Grabber's Coastal Kitchen, **146**

Sol's Sandwich Shop & Deli, **132**

Spinning Wheel, **46**

Steel City Pops, **194**

T
Taj India, **166**

Ted's Restaurant, **184**

The Bright Star, **168**

The Collins Bar, **60**

The Fish Market Southside, **174**

The Gardens Café, **172**

The Great Wall, **82**

The Louis, **70**

The Marble Ring, **54**

The Pita Stop, **88**

V
Vino, **178**

Y
Yo' Mama's Restaurant, **206**

Z
Z's Restaurant, **218**

Zoës Kitchen, **124**

MAGIC CITY CRAVINGS 223

index...

RECIPES

GONE BUT NOT FORGOTTEN FAVORITES

Cinnamon Rolls, Ensley Grill, **44**

Coconut Cake, Marsh Bakery, **28**

Egg Foo Young, Joy Young, **26**

Famous Lemon Icebox Pie, Ed Salem's Drive In, **40**

Famous Stake An' Biskits, Ireland's, **32**

Helen Gulas' Baklava, Gulas' Restaurant, **38**

Nick's Famous Greek Snapper, Rossi's Italian Restaurant, **42**

Peanut Butter Milkshake, Spinning Wheel, **46**

She-Crab Soup, Cobb Lane Restaurant, **34**

Squash Croquettes, Pioneer Cafeteria, **36**

Trout Almandine, John's Restaurant, **30**

COCKTAILS

Alabama Bushwacker Cocktail, Saw's Juke Joint, **62**

Blackberry Mojito, Jinsei, **56**

Bourbon Slush, Dram Whiskey Bar, **52**

Cranberry Champagne Sparkler, Gallery Bar, **66**

Elder-Fashioned, John's City Diner, **68**

Heirloom Blush, Little Savannah Restaurant and Bar,, **72**

Kentucky Apple Cocktail, Brick & Tin, **64**

Lowcountry Peach Daiquiri, Dyron's Lowcountry, **58**

Prepare to be Boarded, The Collins Bar, **60**

Ruby Blue Cocktail, The Louis, **70**

Spirit of Resistance, Roots & Revelry, **74**

The Alabama Songbird, The Collins Bar, **60**

The Land of G Cocktail, The Louis, **70**

Wonderland Cocktail, The Marble Ring, **54**

APPETIZERS & BREADS

Arancini with Sicilian Tomato Sauce, Bottega, **84**

Avo Dip, Avo Restaurant, **98**

Cracklin' Muffins, Rib-It-Up, **92**

Dan Dan Noodle, The Great Wall, **82**

Feta Theologos, Nabeel's Café & Market, **96**

Fire-Baked Chicken Wings, Slice Pizza & Brewhouse, **86**

Hummus, The Pita Stop, **88**

Momos, Bamboo on 2nd, **78**

Pimento Cheese Fritters, Century Restaurant & Bar, **94**

Pork Belly and Fried Oysters, Sky Castle Gastro Lounge, **90**

Tartine Provençale, Chez Fonfon, **80**

SALADS & SIDES

Baby Blue Salad, Homewood Gourmet, **120**

Bottega Bowl, Bottega Café, **104**

Brussels Sprout and Kale Salad, Post Office Pies, **108**

Famous Fried Green Tomatoes, Irondale Café, **118**

Humitas with Charred Herb Salsa, Ovenbird, **116**

Live Med Salad, Zoës Kitchen, **124**

Not Your Mama's Macaroni and Cheese, John's City Diner, **110**

Spinach Salad, Ashley Mac's, **122**

Tomato Salad with Cucumbers, Basil, and Lady Pea Vinaigrette, Highlands Bar and Grill, **102**

Tomato Salad, Hot and Hot Fish Club, 1**12**

SOUPS & SANDWICHES

Baja Shrimp Tacos, Snapper Grabber's Coastal Kitchen, **146**

Butternut Squash Soup, Brick & Tin, **142**

Everything Toast, Revelator Coffee, **140**

George's Oyster Stew, 5 Point Public House, **138**

Grass-Fed Beef Willis Burger, Shindig's Catering & Food Truck, **148**

Hot and Sour Soup, Formosa Hoover Chinese Restaurant, **134**

Hot Beef Sandwich, Gilchrist Sandwich Shop, **136**

Kickback Chicken, Holler & Dash, **130**

Seafood Gumbo, Dyron's Lowcountry, **128**

Super Sol Burger, Sol's Sandwich Shop & Deli, **132**

The Augusta, Busy Corner Cheese & Provisions, **144**

MAIN COURSES

BBQ Pork n'Greens, Saw's Soul Kitchen, **154**

Bar-B-Q Rub, Jim 'N Nick's Bar-B-Q, **164**

Chicken and Prosciutto Pasta, Giuseppe's Café, **186**

Chicken Tikka Masala, Taj India, **166**

Coddled Egg Over Creamy Gulf Shrimp, Satterfield's Restaurant, **180**

Crab Cakes, Little Savannah Restaurant and Bar, **170**

Eggplant Chicken Capellini, Vino, **178**

Flat-Top Roasted Chicken, Miss Dots, **162**

George's Stuffed Rainbow Trout, The Fish Market Southside, **174**

Grilled Whole Gulf Snapper, Ocean, **158**

Moussaka, Nabeel's Café & Market, **190**

Penne alla Vodka, Gianmarco's Restaurant, **160**

Pork Picatta dg, dg, **188**

Pork Shank Silvertron, Silvertron Café, **182**

Shepherd's Pie, Blackwell's Pub & Eatery, **176**

Souvlakia, Ted's Restaurant, **184**

Tenderloin of Beef Greek Style, The Bright Star, **168**

Tomato Pie, The Gardens Café, **172**

DESSERTS

Apple Spice Walnut Cake, Roberts Cuisine, **220**

Carrot Cake with Cream Cheese Icing, Olexa's, **198**

Chocolate Mousse Bombes, Iz Café, **212**

Coconut Cream Pie, Rusty's Bar-B-Q, **210**

Coconut Popsicle, Steel City Pops, **194**

Double Crust Apple Pie, Pie Lab, **216**

Fig and Goat Cheese Ice Cream, Big Spoon Creamery, **204**

Half Moon Cookie, Full Moon Bar-B-Que, **200**

Hummingbird Cake, Birmingham Breadworks, **202**

Niki's Famous Banana Pudding, Niki's West, **196**

Peach Cobbler, Yo' Mama's Restaurant, **206**

Petite Fudge Cakes, Dreamcakes Bakery, **208**

Sweet Potato Pie, Z's Restaurant, **218**

index...
INGREDIENTS

ACAI JUICE
Shindig's Grass-Fed Beef Willis Burger, **148**

ALMONDS
Ashley Mac's Spinach Salad, **122**
John's Restaurant Trout Almandine, **30**

ANCHOVIES
Chez Fonfon Tartine Provençale, **80**

APPLES
Brick & Tin Kentucky Apple Cocktail, **64**
Pie Lab Double Crust Apple Pie, **216**
Roberts Cuisine Apple Spice Walnut Cake, **220**

APRICOT
Silvertron Café Pork Shank Silvertron, **182**

ARUGULA
Revelator Coffee Everything Toast, **140**
Shindig's Grass-Fed Beef Willis Burger, **148**
Sky Castle Pork Belly and Fried Oysters, **90**

ARTICHOKE HEARTS
The Fish Market Southside George's Stuffed Rainbow Trout, **174**

AVOCADOS
Ashley Mac's Spinach Salad, **122**
Avo Dip, **98**
Bottega Bowl, **104**

BACON
Hot and Hot Tomato Salad, **112**
Post Office Pies Brussels Sprout and Kale Salad, **108**
Saw's BBQ Pork n'Greens, **154**
Shindig's Grass-Fed Beef Willis Burger, **148**

BAMBOO SHOOTS
Formosa Hot and Sour Soup, **134**

BANANAS
Birmingham Breadworks Hummingbird Cake, **202**
Niki's Famous Banana Pudding, **196**

BASIL
Hot and Hot Tomato Salad, **112**

BARBECUE
Jim 'N Nick's Bar-B-Q Rub, **164**
Saw's BBQ Pork n'Greens, **154**

BEANS
Zoës Kitchen Live Med Salad, **124**

BEEF (See also: Beef, Ground)
Ireland's Famous Stake An' Biskits, **32**
Ted's Souvlakia, **184**
The Bright Star Tenderloin of Beef Greek Style, **168**

BEEF, GROUND
Blackwell's Shepherd's Pie, **176**
Gilchrist Hot Beef Sandwich, **136**
Nabeel's Moussaka, **190**
Shindig's Grass-Fed Beef Willis Burger, **148**
Sol's Super Soul Burger, **132**

BEER
Dyron's Seafood Gumbo, **128**

BEETS
Bottega Bowl, **104**

BELL PEPPERS
Bottega Bowl, **104**
Century Pimento Cheese Fritters, **94**

Dyron's Seafood Gumbo, **128**
Joy Young Egg Foo Young, **26**
Little Savannah Crab Cakes, **170**
Satterfield's Coddled Egg Over
    Creamy Gulf Shrimp, **180**
The Fish Market Southside George's
    Stuffed Rainbow Trout, **174**

BLACKBERRIES
Jinsei Sushi Blackberry Mojito, **56**

BLEU CHEESE
Homewood Gourmet
    Baby Blue Salad, **120**
Shindig's Grass-Fed
    Beef Willis Burger, **148**

BOURBON
Brick & Tin Kentucky Apple Cocktail, **64**
Dram Bourbon Slush, **52**
The Louis The Land of G Cocktail, **70**

BRANDY
Chez Fonfon Tartine Provençale, **80**
The Collins Bar Prepare to be Boarded, **60**

BREAD CRUMBS
Bottega Arancini with Sicilian
    Tomato Sauce, **84**
John's City Diner Not Your Mama's
    Macaroni and Cheese, **110**
Little Savannah Crab Cakes, **170**
Century Pimento Cheese Fritters, **94**
Pioneer Cafeteria Squash Croquettes, **36**
The Fish Market Southside George's
    Stuffed Rainbow Trout, **174**
Vino Eggplant Chicken Capellini, **178**

BROWN SUGAR
Ensley Grill Cinnamon Rolls, **44**

Full Moon Half Moon Cookie, **200**
Jim 'N Nick's Bar-B-Q Rub, **164**
Roberts Cuisine Apple Spice
    Walnut Cake, **220**

BRUSSELS SPROUTS
Post Office Pies Brussels Sprout
    and Kale Salad, **108**

BUTTERMILK
Brick & Tin Butternut Squash Soup, **142**
Ireland's Famous Stake An' Biskits, **32**
John's Restaurant Trout Almandine, **30**
Olexa's Carrot Cake
    with Cream Cheese Icing, **198**
Rib-It-Up Cracklin' Muffins, **92**
Sky Castle Pork Belly
    and Fried Oysters, **90**

BUTTERNUT SQUASH
Brick & Tin Butternut Squash Soup, **142**

CABBAGE
Snapper Grabber's Baja
    Shrimp Tacos, **146**

CARROTS
Blackwell's Shepherd's Pie, **176**
Bottega Arancini with Sicilian
    Tomato Sauce, **84**
Bottega Bowl, **104**
Highlands Tomato Salad with Cucumbers,
    Basil, and Lady Pea Vinaigrette, **102**
Olexa's Carrot Cake
    with Cream Cheese Icing, **198**
Sky Castle Pork Belly
    and Fried Oysters, **90**

CAPERS
Chez Fonfon Tartine Provençale, **80**

CELERY
Bottega Arancini with
    Sicilian Tomato Sauce, **84**
Cobb Lane She-Crab Soup, **34**
Dyron's Seafood Gumbo, **128**
Joy Young Egg Foo Young, **26**
Satterfield's Coddled Egg Over
    Creamy Gulf Shrimp, **180**
Sky Castle Pork Belly
    and Fried Oysters, **90**

CHEDDAR
Busy Corner Cheese The Augusta, **144**
Century Pimento Cheese Fritters, **94**
Saw's BBQ Pork n'Greens, **154**

CHEESE (See also: Cheddar, Cream Cheese, Feta, Goat Cheese, Mozzarella, Ricotta)
Birmingham Breadworks
    Hummingbird Cake, **202**
Blackwell's Shepherd's Pie, **176**
Century Pimento Cheese Fritters, **94**
Homewood Gourmet
    Baby Blue Salad, **120**
John's City Diner Not Your Mama's
    Macaroni and Cheese, **110**
Nabeel's Moussaka, **190**
Satterfield's Coddled Egg Over
    Creamy Gulf Shrimp, **180**
Snapper Grabber's Baja
    Shrimp Tacos, **146**
The Gardens Café Tomato Pie, **172**
Zoës Kitchen Live Med Salad, **124**

CHAMPAGNE
Gallery Bar Cranberry
    Champagne Sparkler, **90**

CHERRIES
John's City Diner Elder-Fashioned, **68**

CHICKEN
Bottega Bowl, **104**
Giuseppe's Chicken and Prosciutto Pasta, **186**
Holler & Dash Kickback Chicken, **130**
Miss Dots Flat-Top Roasted Chicken, **162**
Slice Fire-Baked Chicken Wings, **86**
Taj India Chicken Tikka Masala, **166**
Vino Eggplant Chicken Capellini, **178**

CHICKPEAS
Bottega Bowl, **104**
The Pita Stop Hummus, **88**

CHIVES
Hot and Hot Tomato Salad, **112**

CHOCOLATE
Dreamcakes Petite Fudge Cakes, **208**
Full Moon Half Moon Cookie, **200**
Iz Café Chocolate Mousse Bombes, **212**

CILANTRO
Avo Dip, **98**
Bamboo on 2nd Momos, **78**
Post Office Pies Brussels Sprout and Kale Salad, **108**

CINNAMON
Ensley Grill Cinnamon Rolls, **44**

COCONUT
Marsh Bakery Coconut Cake, **28**
Olexa's Carrot Cake with Cream Cheese Icing, **198**
Rusty's Coconut Cream Pie, **210**
Steel City Pops Coconut Popsicle, **194**

Taj India Chicken Tikka Masala, **166**
Birmingham Breadworks Hummingbird Cake, **202**

COFFEE
Iz Café Chocolate Mousse Bombes, **212**

CORN
Hot and Hot Tomato Salad, **112**
OvenBird Humitas with Charred Herb Salsa, **112**

CRAB
Cobb Lane She-Crab Soup, **34**
Dyron's Seafood Gumbo, **128**
Little Savannah Crab Cakes, **170**

CRAISINS
Ashley Mac's Spinach Salad, **122**

CRANBERRIES
Gallery Bar Cranberry Champagne Sparkler, **66**

CREAM CHEESE
Century Pimento Cheese Fritters, **94**
Olexa's Carrot Cake with Cream Cheese Icing, **198**
Birmingham Breadworks Hummingbird Cake, **202**

CUCUMBER
Highlands Tomato Salad with Cucumbers, Basil, and Lady Pea Vinaigrette, **102**
Little Savannah Heirloom Blush, **72**

DUMPLING WRAPPERS
Bamboo on 2nd Momos, **78**

EGGS
Bottega Bowl, **104**
Satterfield's Coddled Egg Over Creamy Gulf Shrimp, **180**

EGGPLANT
Nabeel's Moussaka, **190**
Vino Eggplant Chicken Capellini, **178**

FENNEL
OvenBird Humitas with Charred Herb Salsa, **112**

FETA
Ashley Mac's Spinach Salad, **122**
Bottega Bowl, **104**
Nabeel's Feta Theologos, **96**
The Gardens Café Tomato Pie, **172**

FIGS
Big Spoon Creamery Fig and Goat Cheese Ice Cream, **204**
Shindig's Grass-Fed Beef Willis Burger, **148**

GIN
The Louis The Land of G Cocktail, **70**

GINGER
Bamboo on 2nd Momos, **78**

GRITS
Saw's BBQ Pork n'Greens, **154**

GOAT CHEESE
Chez Fonfon Tartine Provençale, 80
Holler & Dash Kickback Chicken, 130

KALE
Post Office Pies Brussels Sprout
  and Kale Salad, 108

LAMB
Ted's Souvlakia, 184

LEMON
Ed Salem's Lemon Icebox Pie, 40
The Marble Ring Wonderland Cocktail, 54

LETTUCE
Bottega Bowl, 104
Homewood Gourmet
  Baby Blue Salad, 120
Snapper Grabber's Baja
  Shrimp Tacos, 146

LIME
Avo Dip, 98
Roots & Revelry Spirit of Resistance, 74

MAYONNAISE
Busy Corner Cheese The Augusta, 144
Sky Castle Pork Belly
  and Fried Oysters, 90
The Gardens Café Tomato Pie, 172

MINT
Jinsei Sushi Blackberry Mojito, 56

Post Office Pies Brussels Sprout
  and Kale Salad, 108

MOZZARELLA
Bottega Arancini with Sicilian
  Tomato Sauce, 84

MUSHROOMS
Cobb Lane She-Crab Soup, 34
Formosa Hot and Sour Soup, 134
Gianmarco's Penne alla Vodka, 160
Joy Young Egg Foo Young, 26
Vino Eggplant Chicken Capellini, 178

NILLA WAFERS
Niki's Famous Banana Pudding, 196

NOODLES
The Great Wall Dan Dan Noodle, 82

OKRA
Hot and Hot Tomato Salad, 112

OLIVES
Chez Fonfon Tartine Provençale, 80

ORANGES
Homewood Gourmet
  Baby Blue Salad, 120
John's City Diner Elder-Fashioned, 68

OYSTERS
5 Point George's Oyster Stew, 138
Sky Castle Pork Belly
  and Fried Oysters, 90

PANCETTA
Gianmarco's Penne alla Vodka, 160

PASTA
Gianmarco's Penne alla Vodka, 160
Giuseppe's Chicken
  and Prosciutto Pasta, 186
John's City Diner Not Your Mama's
  Macaroni and Cheese, 110

PEACHES
Dyron's Lowcountry Peach Daiquiri, 58
Yo' Mama's Peach Cobbler, 206

PEANUT BUTTER
The Spinning Wheel Peanut Butter
  Milkshake, 46

PEAS
Blackwell's Shepherd's Pie, 176
Gianmarco's Penne alla Vodka, 160
Highlands Tomato Salad with Cucumbers,
  Basil, and Lady Pea Vinaigrette, 102
Hot and Hot Tomato Salad, 112

PECANS
Birmingham Breadworks
  Hummingbird Cake, 202
Full Moon Half Moon Cookie, 200
Gulas' Restaurant Helen Gulas'
  Baklava, 38
Homewood Gourmet
  Baby Blue Salad, 120
Pie Lab Double Crust Apple Pie, 216

PEPPERS (See also: Bell Peppers, Jalepenos, Poblanos)
Century Pimento Cheese Fritters, 94

Holler & Dash Kickback Chicken, 130

Ovenbird Humitas with Charred Herb Salsa, 112

PINEAPPLE

Birmingham Breadworks Hummingbird Cake, 202

Olexa's Carrot Cake with Cream Cheese Icing, 198

PHYLLO DOUGH

Gulas' Restaurant Helen Gulas' Baklava, 38

POBLANOS

Avo Dip, 98

Century Pimento Cheese Fritters, 94

Little Savannah Crab Cakes, 170

PORK (See also: BACON, HAM, PANCETTA, PROSCIUTTO, SAUSAGE)

dg Pork Picatta dg, 188

Rib-It-Up Cracklin' Muffins, 92

Saw's BBQ Pork n'Greens, 154

Silvertron Café Pork Shank Silvertron, 182

Sky Castle Pork Belly and Fried Oysters, 90

Ted's Souvlakia, 184

POTATOES (See also: SWEET POTATOES)

Blackwell's Shepherd's Pie, 176

PROSCIUTTO

Giuseppe's Chicken and Prosciutto Pasta, 186

John's City Diner Not Your Mama's Macaroni and Cheese, 110

QUINOA

Bottega Bowl, 104

RADISH

Bottega Bowl, 104

RAISINS

Olexa's Carrot Cake with Cream Cheese Icing, 198

Silvertron Café Pork Shank Silvertron, 182

RICE

Cobb Lane She-Crab Soup, 34

Dyron's Seafood Gumbo, 128

RICOTTA

Revelator Coffee Everything Toast, 140

RISOTTO

Bottega Arancini with Sicilian Tomato Sauce, 84

RUM

Chez Fonfon Tartine Provençale, 80

Dyron's Lowcountry Peach Daiquiri, 58

Jinsei Sushi Blackberry Mojito, 56

Saw's Juke Joint Alabama Bushwacker Cocktail, 62

The Collins Bar Prepare to be Boarded, 60

SAUSAGE

Satterfield's Coddled Egg Over Creamy Gulf Shrimp, 180

SEAFOOD (See also: Crab, Salmon, Oysters, Trout, Scallop, Shrimp, Snapper)

SALMON

Revelator Coffee Everything Toast, 140

SCALLOP

Formosa Hot and Sour Soup, 134

SHRIMP

Dyron's Seafood Gumbo, 128

Formosa Hot and Sour Soup, 134

Joy Young Egg Foo Young, 26

Satterfield's Coddled Egg Over Creamy Gulf Shrimp, 180

Snapper Grabber's Baja Shrimp Tacos, 146

The Fish Market Southside George's Stuffed Rainbow Trout, 174

SNAPPER

Ocean Grilled Whole Gulf Snapper, 158

Rossi's Nick's Famous Greek Snapper, 42

SOY

Formosa Hot and Sour Soup, 134

Bamboo on 2nd Momos, 78

Joy Young Egg Foo Young, 26

Sky Castle Pork Belly and Fried Oysters, 90

The Great Wall Dan Dan Noodle, 82

SPINACH

Ashley Mac's Spinach Salad, 122

The Fish Market Southside George's Stuffed Rainbow Trout, 174

Zoës Kitchen Live Med Salad, 124

SQUASH (See also: Butternut Squash)
Pioneer Cafeteria Squash Croquettes, **36**
Zoës Kitchen Live Med Salad, **124**

STRAWBERRIES
Homewood Gourmet Baby Blue Salad, **120**

SUGAR SNAP PEAS
Bottega Bowl, **104**
Joy Young Egg Foo Young, **26**

SWEET POTATOES
Z's Sweet Potato Pie, **218**

TAHINI
The Pita Stop Hummus, **88**

TEA
Dram Bourbon Slush, **52**

TEQUILA
Roots & Revelry Spirit of Resistance, **74**
The Louis Ruby Blue Cocktail, **70**

TOFU
Formosa Hot and Sour Soup, **134**

TOMATOES (see: Tomatoes, Green)
Avo Dip, **98**
Bamboo on 2nd Momos, **78**
Bottega Arancini with Sicilian Tomato Sauce, **84**
Dyron's Seafood Gumbo, **128**
Highlands Tomato Salad with Cucumbers, Basil, and Lady Pea Vinaigrette, **102**
Hot and Hot Tomato Salad, **112**
Little Savannah Heirloom Blush, **72**
Rossi's Nick's Famous Greek Snapper, **42**
Snapper Grabber's Baja Shrimp Tacos, **146**
The Gardens Café Tomato Pie, **172**
Zoës Kitchen Live Med Salad, **124**

TOMATOES, GREEN
Irondale Cafe Fried Green Tomatoes, **118**

TORTILLAS
Snapper Grabber's Baja Shrimp Tacos, **146**

TROUT
John's Restaurant Trout Almandine, **30**
The Fish Market Southside George's Stuffed Rainbow Trout, **174**

TURKEY
Bamboo on 2nd Momos, **78**

TURNIP GREENS
Saw's BBQ Pork n'Greens, **154**

VANILLA
Big Spoon Creamery Fig and Goat Cheese Ice Cream, **204**
Full Moon Half Moon Cookie, **200**
Marsh Bakery Coconut Cake, **28**
Shindig's Grass-Fed Beef Willis Burger, **148**
Z's Sweet Potato Pie, **218**

VODKA
Gianmarco's Penne alla Vodka, **160**

Little Savannah Heirloom Blush, **72**
The Marble Ring Wonderland Cocktail, **54**

WALNUTS
Olexa's Carrot Cake with Cream Cheese Icing, **198**
Roberts Cuisine Apple Spice Walnut Cake, **220**

WHISKEY
John's City Diner Elder-Fashioned, **68**

WINE (Red)
Vino Eggplant Chicken Capellini, **178**

WINE (White)
dg Pork Picatta dg, **188**
Rossi's Nick's Famous Greek Snapper, **42**

Yogurt
Taj India Chicken Tikka Masala, **166**

Zucchini
Zoës Kitchen Live Med Salad, **124**

where... TO EAT WHAT

After we published *Birmingham's Best Bites*, we got hundreds of inquiries about where to eat what around town, so this time we thought we'd make it easier for you to know where to go for what occasion. Hours of operation and menus may change, so please refer to the individual restaurant or its website for the most current information. Here are our suggestions for restaurants in this book by occasion. - *Martie*

BREAKFAST
The early bird gets the eggs—or the pancakes.
Birmingham Breadworks, **202**
Holler & Dash, **130**
Iz Café, **212**
Niki's West, **196**
Revelator Coffee, **140**
Shindig's Catering & Food Truck, **148**
Silvertron Café, **182**
Sol's Sandwich Shop & Deli, **132**
Ted's Restaurant, **184**

BRUNCH
Where breakfast meets lunch on Saturday or Sunday.
Brick & Tin (Mountain Brook), **64, 142**
Dyron's Lowcountry, **58, 128**
Holler & Dash, **130**
Little Savannah Restaurant and Bar (limited), **72, 170**
OvenBird (in season), **116**
Roberts Cuisine, **220**
Roots & Revelry, **74**
Silvertron Café, **182**
Sky Castle Gastro Lounge, **90**
Yo' Mama's Restaurant (limited), **206**

LADIES WHO LUNCH
Light bites, great atmosphere, and always a sweet ending.
Avo Restaurant, **98**
Bottega Café, **104**
Brick & Tin (Mountain Brook), **64, 142**
Chez Fonfon, **80**
dg, **188**
Gilchrist Sandwich Shop, **136**
Homewood Gourmet, **120**
Iz Café, **212**
Nabeel's Café & Market, **96, 190**
Olexa's, **198**
The Gardens Café, **172**
Zoës Kitchen, **124**

MEAT-AND-THREE
A Birmingham tradition: meat and 3 vegetables for the uninitiated—and by vegetable, we mean mac 'n cheese.
dg, **188**
Irondale Café, **118**
Niki's West, **196**
Sol's Sandwich Shop & Deli, **132**
Ted's Restaurant, **184**
Z's Restaurant, **218**

HAPPY HOUR
After-work spots where there's a cocktail with your name on it.
5 Point Public House, **138**
Avo Restaurant, **98**
Blackwell's Pub & Eatery, **176**
dg, **188**
Gallery Bar, **66**
John's City Diner, **68, 110**
OvenBird, **116**
Roots & Revelry, **74**
Slice Pizza & Brewhouse, **86**
The Louis (The Pizitz Food Hall), **70**

DATE NIGHT
Setting, ambience, and menu perfect for a first date or a night to call a babysitter.
Bamboo on 2nd, **78**
Bottega, **84**
Chez Fonfon, **80**
Gianmarco's Restaurant, **160**
Giuseppe's Café, **186**
Jinsei, **56**
Little Savannah Restaurant and Bar, **72, 170**
OvenBird, **116**
Roots & Revelry, **74**
Silvertron Café, **182**
Steel City Pops, **194**
Taj India, **166**
The Marble Ring, **54**
The Pizitz Food Hall, **70, 144**
Vino, **178**

EXTENSIVE WINE LIST
Where the wine list shines.
Avo Restaurant, **98**
Bottega, **84**
Brick & Tin (Mountain Brook), **64, 142**

dg, **188**
Gianmarco's Restaurant, **160**
Highlands Bar and Grill, **102**
Hot and Hot Fish Club, **112**
Ocean, **158**
Satterfield's Restaurant, **180**
Vino, **178**

LATE NIGHT BITES
Where to go after 9 p.m. in the Magic City.
Bamboo on 2nd, **78**
Dram Whiskey Bar, **52**
OvenBird, **116**
Post Office Pies (weekends), **108**
Saw's Juke Joint, **62**
Sky Castle Gastro Lounge, **90**
The Pizitz Food Hall, **70, 144**

A GREAT BURGER
Notable burgers at places you may not expect to find them.
5 Point Public House, **138**
Chez Fonfon, **80**
Gianmarco's Restaurant, **160**
Jim 'N Nick's Bar-B-Q, **164**
OvenBird, **116**
Rusty's Bar-B-Q, **210**
Saw's Juke Joint, **62**
Saw's Soul Kitchen, **154**
Sky Castle Gastro Lounge, **90**
Shindig's Catering & Food Truck, **148**
Sol's Sandwich Shop & Deli, **132**

LANDMARKS
Buildings with a past and food that stands the test of time.
Century Restaurant & Bar (at the Tutwiler Hotel), **94**
Gilchrist Sandwich Shop, **136**
Highlands Bar and Grill, **102**
John's City Diner, **68, 110**
Niki's West, **196**
Saw's Soul Kitchen, **154**

The Bright Star, **168**
The Gardens Café, **172**
The Pizitz Food Hall, **70, 144**

SUNDAY LUNCH
Something to try after church and beyond.
Miss Dots, **162**
Roberts Cuisine, **220**
Taj India, **166**
The Bright Star, **168**
The Fish Market Southside, **174**
The Pita Stop, **88**
The Pizitz Food Hall, **70, 144**
Z's Restaurant, **218**

GRAB & GO
Find a cooler or freezer of take home favorites.
Ashley Mac's, **122**
Homewood Gourmet, **120**
Iz Café, **212**
Miss Dots, **162**
Nabeel's Café & Market, **96, 190**
Olexa's, **198**
Sol's Sandwich Shop & Deli, **132**
The Pizitz Food Hall, **70, 144**
Zoës Kitchen, **124**

SEAFOOD
Swim in for sushi or seafood.
5 Point Public House, **138**
Bamboo on 2nd, **78**
Chez Fonfon, **80**
dg, **188**
Jinsei, **56**
Ocean, **158**
Snapper Grabber's Coastal Kitchen, **146**
The Bright Star, **168**
The Fish Market Southside, **174**

DECADENT DESSERTS:
House-made sweet endings of note.
Ashley Mac's, **122**
Bottega, **84**

Bottega Café, **104**
Chez Fonfon, **80**
Dreamcakes Bakery, **208**
Highlands Bar and Grill, **102**
Hot and Hot Fish Club, **112**
Ocean, **158**
Olexa's, **198**
Satterfield's Restaurant, **180**
Z's Restaurant, **218**

INSPIRED COCKTAILS
There's nothing unoriginal here.
Brick & Tin (Mountain Brook), **64, 142**
Chez Fonfon, **80**
Dram Whiskey Bar, **52**
Dyron's Lowcountry, **58, 128**
Collins Bar, **60**
Highlands Bar and Grill, **102**
Hot and Hot Fish Club, **112**
Jinsei, **56**
John's City Diner, **68, 110**
Little Savannah Restaurant and Bar, **72, 170**
OvenBird, **116**
Satterfield's Restaurant, **180**
The Collins Bar, **60**
The Marble Ring, **54**

BARBECUE
You're barking up the right tree.
Full Moon Bar-B-Que, **200**
Jim 'N Nick's Bar-B-Q, **164**
Rib-It-Up, **92**
Rusty's Bar-B-Q, **210**
Saw's Juke Joint, **62**
Saw's Soul Kitchen, **154**
Yo' Mama's Restaurant, **206**

FOOD TRUCKS
Creative meals on wheels popping up all around town.
Big Spoon Creamery, **204**
Dreamcakes Bakery, **208**
Shindig's Catering & Food Truck, **148**
Snapper Grabber's Coastal Kitchen, **146**

authors &

MARTIE DUNCAN, Author
Martie Duncan the Chief Party Thrower at MartieDuncan.com, her website dedicated to stress-free entertaining and easy recipes. Martie was runner up on Season 8 of the competition cooking show Food Network Star. She was named the franchise's "Fan Favorite" for the 10th season of the show. Martie spends much of her time on the road, designing and executing weddings and events, as well as speaking at conferences or appearing at culinary shows, charity events, and food festivals. Her how-to videos and party ideas can be found on MyRecipes.com, and she is a food contributor to MSN.com. Her first book, *Birmingham's Best Bites*, features recipes from restaurants, bars, and food trucks around Birmingham. In 2014, Martie, along with co-writer Chanda Temple, was named to an elite list of "20 Women Making a Difference" by *Birmingham Magazine*.

CHANDA TEMPLE, Co-Writer
Chanda Temple is a veteran journalist now working in public relations in Birmingham. No matter the person or the project, she's committed to using public relations to help push a story. In her spare time, she enjoys spending time with family, public speaking, and helping students and adults with writing and networking. Chanda has received numerous awards and recognition for her writing and community work. In 2014, *Birmingham Magazine* selected her as one of the "20 Women Who Make a Difference." In 2013, she received a Distinguished Leadership Award for Excellence in Communications. Also in listed in 2013, she was listed in the publication "Social Media Stars of Birmingham." She blogs about how to be better in careers and more at chandatemplewrites.com

FRANK COUCH, Photographer Frank's passion for documenting daily life through the lens began with the encouragement and guidance of Loretta Gordon, a high school teacher at Ramsay High School. Mentors at The University of Montevallo helped him land an internship at the state's largest daily newspaper that would launch a career documenting the people, places, and things that make Alabama such a unique and diverse place to call home. His work has appeared in several newspapers, magazines, tabloids, and books and has won awards from the Associated Press and Alabama Press Association.

AMY CASH, Calligrapher Amy Cash is the owner of Storied Script Calligraphy. She specializes in wedding calligraphy and custom watercolor maps. You can see more of her work at storiedscript.com.

ELIZABETH CHICK, Graphic Designer Elizabeth Chick is a veteran graphic artist who has worked in her field on-and-off for close to 40 years (she started in kindergarten!). She has designed numerous magazines and books including *Birmingham Magazine*, Hoover Chamber of Commerce guides, Huntsville Chamber of Commerce guides, and Alabama and Auburn championship books. She currently works at Cahaba Media Group as art director for two monthly magazine publications.

contributors

MOESIA (MO) DAVIS, Photographer Mo is an Alabama native. She fell in love with photography at a young age and has had a camera by her side ever since. Mo has styled hundreds of food photos in her career and shot much of *Birmingham's Best Bites* as a photographer for Arden Photography. She shoots many of Birmingham's social occasions and charity events. Wedding photography is her specialty.

RACHEL LOCKHART, Intern Editorial Assistant, Photographer, Photo Editor Rachel is a graduate of Birmingham-Southern College with a love of food and fine art photography. She recently spent time cooking in restaurants in Atlanta to refine her skills in the kitchen before bringing her talent to *Magic City Cravings*.

MADOLINE MARKHAM, Editor After receiving a master's in journalism from the University of Missouri, Madoline returned to Birmingham to pursue her love of all things edible and editorial at *Southern Living*. Her passion for her hometown and its people then led her to write and serve as managing editor for community newspapers and later *B-Metro* magazine. Needless to say, helping bring this book to life was the perfect fusion of her interests, and she's excited to both share it and cook from it.

LISA MITCHELL, Graphic Designer Lisa has been a graphic artist for over 15 years and currently works at the Birmingham Public Library, where she helped design and produce *Birmingham's Best Bites* in 2014. Lisa dedicated many hours to design ideas for *Magic City Cravings*.

DR. JOYCE PETTIS, Copy Editor Dr. Joyce Pettis, formerly a professor of English at North Carolina State University, is a writer and editor in her retirement. She lives in Huntsvillle, Alabama, and also edited *Birmingham's Best Bites*.

ARDEN WARD UPTON, Photographer Arden shot her first wedding in 1999. Eighteen years later, Arden Photography has grown, specializing in celebrations, portraits, and commercial and editorial photography where food has long been her specialty. Her recent collection of equestrian inspired prints launched to rave reviews and can be seen in art galleries across the country. An equestrienne, Arden recently won her first horse showing riding for Windwood Equestrian, the Birmingham area horse farm and wedding venue she owns and manages with her husband, William. Arden gives time to multiple charity projects in Birmingham and donated all the photography for *Birmingham's Best Bites* as well as much of the beautiful photography for this book.